Lost Treasures

GOOD LUCK AND GOOD HUNTING

Gerard Oak

Author: Gerard Oak
Self-Publishing Support: Intertype
45/125 Highbury Road
BURWOOD VIC 3125
Australia
www.intertype.com.au

Book layout by: Intertype
Printed in Australia by: Intertype

Ordering Information:
Quantity sales. Special discounts are available on quantity purchases by corporations, associations, and others. For details, contact the "Special Sales Department" c/- Intertype at the address above.

Lost Treasures / Gerard Oak. —1st ed.
ISBN 978-0-6485960-1-1

Contents

Dedicated to Athena, a man's best friend.

Fortune favours the bold.

—LATIN PROVERB

Introduction

The call of history and archaeology, and the physical 'treasures' that are often associated with it, have entertained me for my entire life. As a child I would bury a jar of coins just to dig them back up months later. Indeed, every little item washed up on the beach or glimpsed under the ocean was analysed by a curious eye, the origin of every bone in the wild was guessed at and the classics such as *Treasure Island* and *The Count of Monte Cristo* were read over and again for inspiration.

As time wore on, however, I noticed that the dreams of lost civilisations, sunken shipwrecks, treasure caves and the secret hideouts of outlaws did not abate. If anything, as I began to travel and experience the world, these dreams grew. With today's access to seemingly unlimited information at your fingertips, and the ability to travel like never before, the time has never been more right to chase history.

This book is the tip of the iceberg on your way to a life of adventure. Ten treasures spread throughout the world that have been lost to time, but not without hope of return. Ten historical targets that are all within *your* reach. Neither are these treasures sunk too deep, aged beyond the reach of written record or guarded too heavily by the earth. A little planning and a sprinkle of luck is all the recipe you need.

Before you begin – A warning. The information you read in the following pages is bathed in the theory, circumstance and ideology of all those who have tried and failed before you. Nothing is gospel, nothing is fact, until you make it so. The realm of treasure hunting leads to disappointment far more often than she leads to glory – but then all the greater the glory.

Good luck and good hunting.

CHAPTER 1

King John Loses his Crown Jewels in the Wash

King John, the infamous thirteenth century ruler of England, has never been treated kindly by historians. True to form, on the 12th of October in the year 1216, an error in judgment caused John to lose his kingdom's crown jewels, as well as various other treasures estimated to be worth over **$70,000,000** today.

King John has been described as 'fiery haired and barrel-chested' and teased by the French for his love of bad-tasting wine.

Important pieces of The Crown Jewels of the United Kingdom, kept in the Tower of London. The history of the vast royal collection is turbulent, with many items also melted down and sold off after the 1649 republican victory over Charles I. Given King John's known love of jewels, his collection would have been impressive.

Amid a campaign to suppress an uprising by his Barons that was supported by France and Scotland, King John was travelling from King's Lynn to Lincoln in England's east. Having received news that the Scottish King, Alexander II, had invaded the northern border, and having contracted dysentery while staying at King's Lynn, John was understandably in a hurry while fighting diarrhea, nausea, vomiting and fits of untrustworthy flatulence.

The weary travelers came to a place on the River Nene near Sutton Bridge, Norfolk, where John decided to save time and send the slower moving baggage trains on a short cut. The horse drawn carts were sent across a usually usable area at low tide. This section at the converging mouth of several rivers had been known as 'The Wash' since Roman times, due to the unusually fast incoming North Sea tide that could reportedly outrun a galloping horse… And that it did. A fierce incoming tide caught the slow-moving train unawares, destroying the carts and drowning the poor men and horses. The royal treasures of the King were lost and, 800 years later, they remain so.

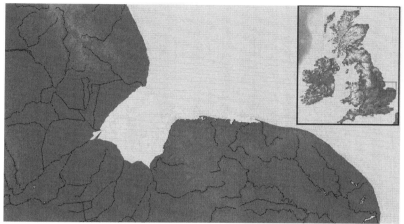

'The Wash' on the east coast of England.

Who was 'Bad' King John?

King John, known to most of us the bad guy in the Robin Hood films, was born on Christmas Eve in 1166, the youngest of five sons to King Henry II. John is described as short, barrel-chested and with dark red hair. He liked reading, gambling, hunting, wearing fancy clothes, extramarital affairs, drinking bad wine (according to French chroniclers) and collecting jewels. John reportedly had an enormous collection of jewels, a hobby that adds enthusiasm to the hunt for his lost riches.

John grew up watching his older brothers launch failed rebellions against the Crown time and again, and by the time their father had died in 1189, only he and the older Richard I remained as heirs. The more imposing Richard the Lionheart was anointed King, but soon after went off crusading in the Holy Lands. This left John at home to scheme unsuccessfully against the royal administration. Despite this, when Richard died in 1199, John was the seen as the rightful heir and became the King of England.

Within a few years, through a combination of negligence, poorly treating his nobles and lack of military preparation, John had lost all English lands in France, was excommunicated by the Pope and faced rising resistance from at home. In an effort to appease the nobility, John signed the *Magna Carta* at Runnymede in 1215, but it was to be a stopgap as neither side were prepared to take this early attempt at England's constitution seriously just yet. Civil war broke out, with the rebellious nobles supported by King Louis VIII of France. It was during this war that John found himself in the east of the country, with a serious bout of dysentery, having just lost the Crown Jewels and seemingly about to lose the war. John died in bed on the 19th of October, 1216, having made it to Newark Castle but unable to travel further.

John was succeeded by his son, the nine-year-old Henry III, under the guidance of the renowned William Marshall, Earl of Pembroke. The noble's rebellion was defeated, and John's royal line secured, albeit in need of a new set of heirlooms.

What was lost?

There is great conjecture about what was lost during the disaster in The Wash, but most historians agree there was a significant amount of royal gold, coins and various royal regalia in the entourage. Less conservative (and more interesting) estimates include the English Crown Jewels, silver plates, gold goblets, a solid gold scepter, the sword of Tristan (a hero from the King Arthur legends) and enough gold coin to literally bathe in.

The Wash

On the east coast of England where Norfolk meets Lancashire, there is a square shaped bay and estuary known playfully as '*The Wash*'. One of the largest estuaries in the United Kingdom, it is fed by the rivers Witham, Welland, Nene and Great Ouse. This is particularly dangerous during a full or new moon, as the North Sea rises and rages back in to take its revenge on the land. Water flows up river violently and floods the low-lying areas, often taking travelers by surprise at placing them at great peril.

The geography of the area is vastly different today than it was during King John's era. Even further back in time, the Vikings had used The Wash to travel inland and capture towns unaware. Nowadays, after 500 years of reclamation efforts and due to the natural course of events, much of the area has been tamed into farmland, particularly the areas that King John's men would have attempted to cross.

Farmland reclaimed from The Wash

. The east bank of the River Nene at Sutton Bridge.

Where to Look

The secret to this lost treasure hasn't remained so due to lack of trying. Locals in the area have been searching for clues with increasing fervour in the 21st century. The advent of more and more advanced technology including metal detectors, laser survey techniques, GPS and even consultation with mediums and Tarot card readers has kept treasure seekers keen on the hunt.

Like so many of the world's great lost treasures, I believe a fresh perspective is going to be the key. It is my sincere hope that an aspiring young Indiana Jones, metal detector in-hand on their day off school, searches a yet unexplored section around Sutton Bridge in *The Wash*, and stumbles across King John's jewel studded royal crown in the knee-high mud. The King is dead... Long live the King!

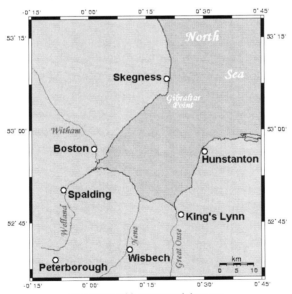

Head here with your metal detector.

CHAPTER 2

The Lost Tomb of Alexander the Great

Somehow, we have managed to lose Alexander the Great. That's right, despite several historical accounts and countless theories, the final resting place of the Macedonian conqueror has not been precisely known for over 2000 years. For the lucky ones that do find the tomb of Alexander, there promises archaeological acclaim that would shine a light on antiquity and make Tutankhamen look like a mummy's boy.

Alexander was born in 356 BC in the Kingdom of Macedon, a powerful empire led by his father, Phillip II. None other than the famous philosopher Aristotle personally tutored Alexander until the age of sixteen, instilling a respect for knowledge and culture that would remain with the young prince. When Alexander was twenty years old, Phillip was assassinated and the heir apparent inherited a wealthy kingdom with a battle-hardened army. Already an experienced commander, in 334 BC Alexander and his trusted generals began what would be ten years of campaigning that would see his empire stretch from the Adriatic Sea to the Indus River (Greece to Pakistan).

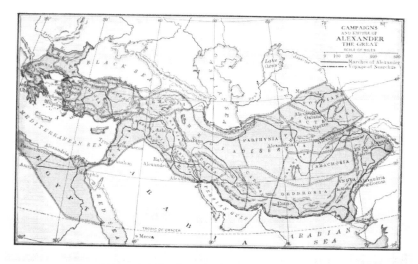

Map of Alexander's Empire at the time of his death in 323 BC.

Action shot of Alexander riding into battle with his mighty steed, Bucephalus.

Alexander's bucket list included the unification of Greece, total conquest of the vast Persian Empire, liberation of Egypt and an invasion of the Indian subcontinent – feats which led to Alexander amassing an enormous amount of wealth and power.

Unfortunately for the great man, in June of 323 BC, aged just thirty-two years of age and having already waged twenty undefeated military campaigns and survived a raft of injuries and close calls, Alexander died of an unknown illness or poisoning after entertaining guests in Babylon. There is one report that the he fell ill after downing an enormous amount of wine at a drunken party; other suggestions include strychnine poisoning, fever, typhoid and liver disease (by all accounts the Macedonians didn't shy away from a big night out).

The Death of Alexander by Karl Piloty (1886).

Where art thou, Alexander?

After the death of the great King, the funeral and burial plans were thrown into disarray and began centuries of uncertainty as to the whereabouts of Alexander's final resting place. Based on contemporary sources, we can use use the following points to establish a time line of events post mortem, including theories and clues as to the location of his tomb:

General Confusion / Confused Generals

Alexander was placed in a gold sarcophagus filled with honey, which was then placed inside a gold casket. According to Strabo (64 BC – 24 AD), the tradition in Babylon at the time of Alexander's death was for the dead to be buried in a casing of honey or wax.

In the two years after his death in Babylon, Alexander's body was embalmed, and a golden chariot was built to transfer his body. Eventually, with the body and procession finally prepared, the march from the sanctuary of Amun in Babylon began; this was reportedly in accordance with Alexander's own wishes. The chariot was followed by military guards and soldiers who opened the path for the great procession.

A reconstruction of Alexander's funeral cortege based on the description from Diodorus Siculus.

Ancient writers Pausanias (AD 110 – 180) and Diodorus Siculus (c. 30 BC) tell us that while the funeral cortege was on its way to Macedonia and crossing the border of Syria and Egypt, Ptolemy Soter (one of Alexander's leading generals and founder of the Egyptian Ptolemaic dynasty) seized the procession and then buried Alexander in Memphis, the administrative centre of Egypt at the time. It should be noted that it was also considered a prerequisite for successors to have possession of the prior ruler's body as a symbol of legitimacy – the Egyptians had already recognised Alexander as their pharaoh when he defeated the Persians and liberated them; Sneaky Soter knew what he was doing.

While Ptolemy (toh-lah-mee) was in possession of Alexander's body and sarcophagus, other prominent generals (namely Perdiccas and Eumenes), allegedly relieved Alexander of some armor, his crown and his royal scepter as symbols of their legitimacy as rulers.

According to Plutarch (AD 46 – 120), an oracle had indicated Alexander should be buried in Alexandria. The sarcophagus was soon relocated to the Egyptian city on the Mediterranean; the first and greatest of the twenty cities that bore his name.

Pausanius says Alexander was moved from Memphis by Ptolemy's successor, Ptolemy II Philadelphus, and that Ptolemy IV Philopater eventually placed him in a purpose built Sema (or Soma - meaning body). Zenobius (c. AD 120) relates thus:

> *'Ptolemy Philopater built in the middle of the city a tomb, which is now called the Sema, and he laid there all his forefathers together with his mother, and also Alexander the Macedonian.'*

Diodorus Siculus, the most contemporary of our sources, confirms Zenobius' statement, albeit without specifying which 'Ptolemy' was responsible, but you get the idea:

'Ptolemy devised a sacred precinct, which in size and construction was worthy of Alexander's glory.'

The tomb became a focal point for the Ptolemaic cult of Alexander the Great. In his famous work titled Geographica, Strabo tells us of the tomb or Sema, located within the royal section of the city:

'The Sema also, as it is called, is a part of the royal palaces. This was the enclosure which contained the burial places of the Kings and that of Alexander; for Ptolemy, the son of Lagus, forestalled Perdiccas by taking the body away from him when he was bringing it down from Babylon and was turning aside towards Egypt, moved by greed and a desire to make that country his own... and the body of Alexander was carried off by Ptolemy and given sepulture in Alexandria, where it still now lies – not, however, in the same sarcophagus as before, for the present one is made of glass, whereas the one wherein Ptolemy laid it was made of gold.'

Strabo provides us with excellent details of the layout of the ancient city, and also describes the actions of Ptolemy X, surely one of the most unpopular rulers Egypt has seen. After having murdered his own mother and co-regent (Cleopatra III – after she was responsible for securing him the throne), Ptolemy X was exiled by his own citizens and army. He fled to Syria but returned with a mercenary army and seized power - an army he then paid for by melting down Alexander's gold sarcophagus and replacing it with a glass one!

This act so enraged the Alexandrians that they again exiled Ptolemy X and attempted to remove all record of him; the fool was later murdered when caught fleeing to Cyprus.

Ptolemy I   Ptolemy IV   Ptolemy X

Referring to this that and the other Ptolemy is a little confusing, but as far our time line goes, the year is now around 100 BC and we have good reason to believe Alexander is resting peacefully in his Egyptian tomb, albeit in a newer, slightly more 'economical' sarcophagus.

False Starts

The recent discovery of a large tomb in northern Greece, at Amphipolis and dating from the time of Alexander, has given rise to speculation that its original intent was to be his burial place. This would fit with the intended destination of Alexander's initial funeral cortege. However, most experts agree that available historical records all mention Alexandria in Egypt as the last known location of Alexander's body.

The so-called "Alexander Sarcophagus", discovered near Sidon and now in the Istanbul Archaeology Museum, is so named not because it was thought to have contained Alexander's remains, but because its bas-relief artwork depicts Alexander and his companions fighting the Persians and hunting. The museum is packed full of remarkable artefacts and well worth a visit if you find yourself in Istanbul (so many treasures that they can't fit them all inside – you can sit in the garden café literally surrounded by timeless pieces of history).

The Alexander Sarcophagus housed in the Istanbul Archaeology Museum.

Romans Emperors, an Egyptian Queen & a Huge Tsunami

Alexander remained in Alexandria until at least late antiquity, having been revered and visited by numerous Roman heads of state including Pompey around 48 BC (after fleeing his rival Julius Caesar), and Caesar himself during his time securing the Egyptian throne for a young Cleopatra (amongst other pastimes with the alluring queen bee).

In 30 BC, Cleopatra is said to have taken gold from Alexander's tomb, to finance her and new beau Marc Antony's war against Octavian (Caesar's nephew and soon to be crowned Emperor Augustus). Having already defeated Antony's forces at Actium, Augustus met little resistance on his arrival in Alexandria and, after Antony and Cleopatra's suicides (and subsequent burial together), he requested to visit the mausoleum of Alexander. In a comical turn of events, the African consul and historian, Cassius Dio (c. 155 – 235 AD), tells of the encounter between Augustus and his idol;

'As he bent over the body to kiss the great conqueror, Augustus accidentally broke Alexander's nose. When Augustus was asked if he wanted to visit the tombs of the Ptolemies, he refused, saying that, 'I came to see a king and not dead people.'

Augustus at the Tomb of Alexander, by Sebastien Bourdon in 1683.

Having had the body brought out of the tomb for a viewing, Augustus reportedly placed a gold diadem and flowers on the body of Alexander, a touching tribute between conquerors that would ironically signal the beginning of almost 700 years of Roman rule.

Suetonius (c. 69 – 122 AD) reports that the mad Emperor Caligula (reigned 37 – 41 AD) visited Alexander and stole his breast plate armour - very disrespectful behaviour from the 'mad one' to the 'great one'.

Emperor Septimius Severus closed the tomb off around the year 200 AD; said to be on or adjacent the ancient crossroads in the centre of the city, it was apparently due to concerns for public safety amidst the hordes of visitors. The emperor was also reported to have placed in the mausoleum many secret books for safe-keeping, the content of which remains a mystery, though it is unlikely they have survived (unless they were stored well or made of something sturdier than papyrus). Many other sources also place the tomb in the ancient city centre. Unfortunately for us, Alexandria has been rebuilt and changed so much since, that we don't know for certain where the original centre was. Strabo again lends us a hand here;

> *'The most important of the latitudinal streets was that of the Sema, which had on its right the tomb of Alexander the Great, and, on its left, very probably the museum. Then it crossed the Canopic Avenue, passed the Adrianum and Caesareum on the right, the temple of Isis-Plousia and the Emporium on the left, and ends on the quay of the great maritime port and the place of embarkation, near the two obelisks.'*

Severus' son and successor, the much-maligned Emperor Caracalla, believed he was the reincarnation of Alexander (reports Herodian c. 170-240 AD). Caracalla was known to visit the tomb during his reign (198 to 217 AD), making what was apparently the last recorded imperial visit and offering his tunic, ring, belt and other jewellery to adorn the resting place. Ironically, Caracalla sacked Alexandria in 215 AD, but is said to have left Alexander in peace.

Unfortunately, others attacked Alexandria, they included Claudius II (269 AD), Aurelian (273 AD) and Diocletian (296 AD), culminating in a repression of the population that almost destroyed the city. There was no reported damage to Alexander's tomb during these attacks. However, the scholarly soldier Ammianus Marcellinus (c. 325-400 AD), in his Res Gestae, wrote that Aurelian had decimated the Bruchium district during a rebellion, and that it remained in ruins as of the mid-fourth century – Bruchium was the region of palaces along the eastern shore of the Great Harbour, also thought by certain scholars to be the area known as the *Royal Quarter*, containing the palaces and *Sema*.

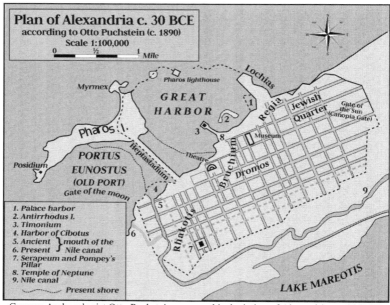

German Archaeologist Otto Puchstein gave us this depiction of Alexandria ca. 30 BCE.

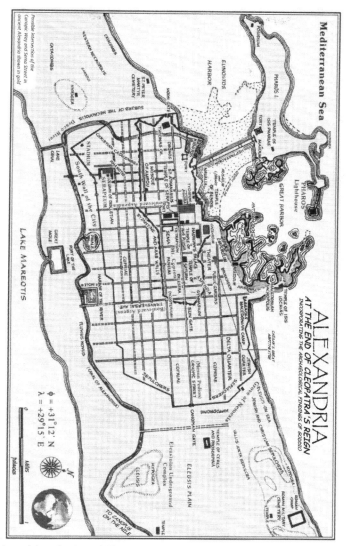

Alexandria at the time of Cleopatra (around 30 BC), with archaeological findings superimposed, by modern day French archaeologist, Franck Goddio.

Natural disasters have also taken a toll on Alexandria. Along with numerous earthquakes over time (estimates of at least twenty-three struck the Egyptian coast between 320-1303 AD), a tsunami in 365 AD caused extensive damage to the city, in particular to the Royal Quarter and the Pharos (a lighthouse one hundred metres tall and a wonder of the ancient world). Some 50,000 homes were destroyed and the shoreline was permanently altered, ensuring the Mediterranean Sea slowly but surely engulfed the Royal Quarter (rediscovered in 1995, the floor of Alexandria's Great Harbour was found to have dropped twenty feet). It is hard to imagine the mausoleum was left unscathed.

Alexandria Harbour after 2000 years of battling man, nature and time... What secrets are submerged in her depths? The Citadel of Qaitbay now stands where the Pharos once shined, and royal palaces, temples and tombs are waiting to be discovered beneath the lapping Mediterranean Sea.

The newly converted Roman Christians under Emperor Theodosius (379-395 AD) may have spelled trouble for the tomb. It is around the turn of the fourth century that paganism was effectively outlawed by the Romans. The Serapeum, a type of large pagan temple, was destroyed and, if this trend continued throughout the city, could be why a previously vener-

ated mausoleum in the centre of the city then slipped away from history.
Indeed, when John Chrysostom, the Archbishop of Constantinople, visited
Alexandria in 400 AD, he asked to see Alexander's tomb, apparently
without success for he remarked:

> *'His tomb even his own people know not.'*

The renowned theologian, Theodoret (c. 393–466 AD), also includes
Alexander in a mid-fifth century list of famous historical figures whose
tombs had by that time become unknown.

Muslims and Mamelukes

We've reached the start of the fifth century and it seems we may have
now definitely lost Alexander the Great... But wait, the Muslim conquest
of Egypt beckons and, after a few hundred years, we begin to hear whis-
pers of the Macedonian once more...

In 641 AD a Muslim army conquered the Byzantine stronghold of Alexandria, the last post of resistance in Egypt. The Muslim commander,
Amr ibn al-As, wrote to his Caliph after the victory:

> *'We have conquered Alexandria. In this city there are 4,000 palaces, 400
> places of entertainment, and untold wealth.'*

No mention of Alexander's tomb... Take heart in the fact that the
Muslim occupiers seemed to have respected the inhabitants of Alexandria
and moved into the homes vacated by the conquered Byzantines - there is
no mention of wholesale destruction or looting. Could it be that by the
year 641 AD the tomb of Alexander the Great had slipped from memory?
Or perhaps beneath the sea, as was the fate of the Royal Quarter after the
tsunami of 365 AD?

There's a glimmer of hope as the ninth and tenth century Muslim authors Ibn Abd al-Hakam (b. AD 803), and Al-Masudi (b. AD 896), report having seen Alexander's Tomb. In the ninth century, Ibn Abd al-Hakam mentions the Mosque of Dalkarnein, positioned near the Gate of Alexandria. Dalkarnein is a transliteration of Zulqarnayn, meaning 'he of two horns', a hero from the Quran who is empowered by Allah to erect a wall between mankind and Gog and Magog, the personifications of chaos. In the Islamic tradition, during the apocalypse Gog and Magog would be released, signaling the end of the world and the Day of Resurrection. Scholars largely agree that this Zulqarnayn (Dalkarnein) is based on Alexander the Great, hence the reverence shown by Muslims to him as a hero in the Quran. Al-Masudi in the middle of the tenth century wrote:

> *'And his burial place made of marble, known as the tomb of Alexander, remains in situ in the city of Alexandria in the country of Egypt to this day.'*

The Mamelukes (slave soldiers ironically loyal to their ex-slave rulers) won control of Alexandria and established a dynasty, ruling Egypt from 1250 – 1517. During their reign, in October 1365, Peter I of Cyprus, under the guise of a religious 'Crusade', occupied and sacked the Mameluke Sultanate in Alexandria, reportedly killing 20,000 and enslaving 5,000 of the inhabitants. For three days Peter's coalition looted the city, targeting mosques, temples, churches and libraries.

There is no specific mention of Alexander's Tomb during the assault.

The Ottoman Turks then conquered Egypt and Alexandria in 1517 but allowed the local Mameluke population to go about their business without a great deal of bother.

The famous Arab historian dubbed Leo Africanus (1494 – 1552), visited Alexandria as a young man and wrote in his Description of Africa in 1526:

> *'It should not be omitted, that in the middle of the city amongst the ruins may be seen a little house in the form of a chapel, in which is a tomb much honoured by the Mahometans; since it is asserted that within it is kept the corpse of Alexander the Great, grand prophet and King, as may be read in the Koran. And many strangers come from distant lands to see and venerate this tomb, leaving at this spot great and frequent alms.'*

The Spanish chronicler, Luis del Marmol Carvajal (1520 – 1600), wrote almost the exact same passage in his work, Descripcion General de Africa:

> *'In the middle of the city, among its ruins, is a small edifice in the form of a chapel; where there is a sepulchre, which the Mahometans hold in great reverence; because they say, that Alexander the Great, Escander, is there buried, whom they worship as a King and a Prophet, and mention in their Alcoran, and, through devotion, resort to it from afar.'*

It is interesting to note that, according to contemporary historians, the local Muslim population revered Alexander, thus would also have protected his resting place.

In 1575, this Map of Alexandria was published by Braun and Hogenberg in Civitates Orbis Terrarum (Historic Cities). It shows a large building with the inscription 'Domus Alexandri Magni' (House of Alexander the Great) in the centre.

Tomb Tourism

An English traveller, George Sandys, visited Alexandria in 1611, and was shown a sepulchre there, venerated as the resting place of Alexander, of which he wrote:

> *'Within a serraglio called Somia, belonging to the palaces, the Ptolemies had their sepulchres, together with Alexander the Great,*
>
> *There is yet here to be seene a little Chappell; within, a Tombe, much honoured and visited by the Mahometans, where they bestow their almes; supposing his body to lie in that place: Himself reputed a great prophet, they being so informed by their Alcoran.'*

One could read two locations into Sandys' description above. It seems the first lines refer to a communal Ptolemaic burial place, and the ensuing lines rather describe an individual chapel.

Dr Richard Pococke of Oxford University visited Alexandria in the mid-eighteenth century and, due to his attempts being thwarted by suspicious locals, didn't see the inside of a tomb for himself, but writes the following of its location in his Description of the East:

> 'The palace, with the suburbs belonging to it, was a fourth part of the city; within its district was the Museum, or Academy, and the burial-place of the kings, where the body of Alexander was deposited in a coffin of gold.'

Pococke uses repeated past tense here;

> 'Was a fourth part of the city' 'Where the body of Alexander was deposited'.
>
> Is the 'fourth part of the city' (referred to in the past tense) actually the sunken Royal Quarter?

Numerous accounts that don't mention Alexander specifically but nonetheless do mention a significant tomb, read as follows...

In The Travels of Egmont and Heyman (1759), the authors describe a magnificent Soma, a sanctuary enclosed within what later became a Christian church:

> 'Here is also a large structure, said to have still within it stately piazzas of Corinthian pillars; but Turks only are permitted to enter it. Nor is it safe for a Christian to come near the walls; so that nothing can be said of it with certainty.'

Egmont and Heyman went on to describe a structure guarded at all times; entry by means of even the most substantial bribe was refused.

In Irwin's Series of Adventures, Eyles Irwin claims in 1777 to have visited a secret tomb within the Church of St. Athanasius (now the Attarine Mosque), without the acquiescence of the locals, of course. Having procured a key by devious means, Irwin gains entry and describes his visit to the said tomb:

> 'We soon came to an ancient temple, a part of which is still habitable, and has been long appropriated to the service of Mahomet. On this account we found some difficulty to obtain admittance. But the key was at length procured by our janissary, and we were shown into the neglected quarter. This is a square of very large diameter, which is surrounded with triple rows of granite pillars of the Corinthian order. These pillars are lofty, and support a roof which is still in a good state of preservation.
>
> The inside of the walls of this temple is inlaid with tables of marble of various colours, which, for their richness and novelty, cannot but engage the admiration of a stranger. In the area of the square is a stone cistern of very antique mould. It is inscribed on all sides with hieroglyphics, and, from a rail which enclosed it, appears to have served for some religious purpose.'

There are third, fourth and fifth examples of such a tomb as given by C.S. Sonnini (1780), W.G. Browne (1792) and two of Napoleon's academics, Denon and Delomieux (1798), during the three-year French occupation of Egypt (1798-1801).

The location of this tomb is given as the Church of St. Athanasius, later to become the Attarine Mosque. Although the existence of this tomb does seem likely and has been the basis for many searches in the modern era, it does not match the description given by earlier, more contemporary chroniclers, and indeed appears to house an empty sarcophagus, giving rise to further theories that Alexander's body may have been removed.

Courtyard of the Attarine Mosque - drawn by French artist and archaeologist Vivant Denon in 1798. Denon was appointed as the first Director of the Louvre museum by Napoleon after the Egyptian campaign.

The Modern Era: Alexandria becomes French, then British, then Egyptian Again

The French arrived and occupied Alexandria in 1798 and, after their fleet was destroyed by the British under Admiral Nelson, either decided or were forced to stay for the next three years. In 1801 the British, having expelled the French from Cairo, laid siege to Alexandria. The French surrendered soon after during the 'Capitulation of Alexandria', sparing the prospect of the city becoming a battle field. The same is said of the brief British occupation of the city in 1807, before they were kindly 'allowed to leave' by the ruling Egyptian dictator, Mohammed Ali.

Created by Napoleon's engineers, this map was a part of the collective works of about 160 scholars and scientists, 2000 artists, 400 engravers and numerous technicians, a collaboration titled 'Description de l'Egypte'.

It was upon the 'Capitulation of Alexandria' that the British acquired the famous Rosetta Stone from the French; by cloak and dagger no doubt as the French were not willing to part with such a treasure. The inscribed stone, the key through which Egyptian hieroglyphs would finally be understood, remains in the British Museum to this day.

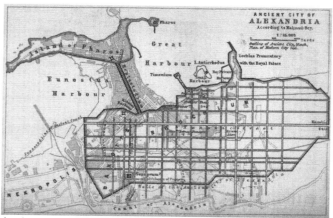

Egyptian Astronomer Mahmoud Bey el-Falaki (1815-1885), produced a map of ancient Alexandria and believed Alexander's tomb lay in the centre, at the intersection of Via Canopica (modern day Horreya Avenue) and the ancient street labelled R5. Several other scholars including Tassos Neuroutsos, Heinrich Kiepert and Ernst von Seiglin place the tomb in the same area.

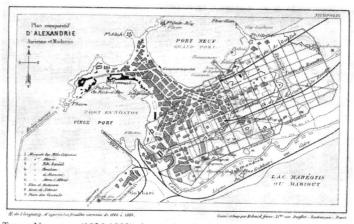

Tassos Neurotsos (1826-1892) also produced a map to accompany his work titled L'Ancienne Alexandrie, published in 1888. The map was based on the earlier Mahmoud Bey version, however included additional details of archaeological investigations and ancient sources.

Alexander Found? ... Not Just Yet

1879, inside the Nabi Daniel Mosque of Alexandria, it is reported that a stone worker accidentally broke through to a vaulted chamber inside the basement of the mosque. Some granite monuments with an angular summit were discovered, but the entrance was then walled-up and the stone worker was asked not to disclose the incident (some historic images show the Alexandrian mausoleum as a building with a pyramidal roof).

In 1888 Heinrich Schliemann (made famous for supposedly rediscovering the city of Troy from Homer's Iliad and planting the fraudulent 'Priam's Treasure'), attempted to locate the tomb within the Nabi Mosque, but he was apparently denied permission to excavate.

Andrew Chugg has a fascinating theory concerning the whereabouts of the Macedonian King, and it's not in Alexandria. Chugg claims Alexander the Great's body was stolen from Alexandria by Venetian merchants in the ninth century, who mistakenly believed him to be Saint Mark the Evangelist. They smuggled the remains to Venice, where they have since been venerated as the remains as Saint Mark in the Basilica Cattedrale Patriarcale di San Marco.

Chugg makes a very good circumstantial argument, citing numerous historic sources and suggesting that as Alexander tomb references seem to dissipate around the end of the fourth century, so appears the tomb of Saint Mark in the same area of the Alexandria – allegedly containing the body of the Saint that was later removed by Venetian merchants. There are numerous other connections pointed out on his website and well worth a read.

Greek Archaeologist, Liana Souvaltzi, claims she discovered the tomb over twenty years ago, but has been blocked by the Egyptian and Greek governments ever since. Souvaltzi also makes an excellent argument for having located Alexander, this time in the Siwa Oasis area, between the Qattara Depression and the Egyptian Sand Sea in the Libyan Desert. From

1989 to 1995 the archaeologist and her team uncovered a spectacular 525 square meter Hellenistic royal tomb. Once again, many clues equate the tomb with that of Alexander, including the symbols of Amun Ra (the equivalent of Zeus – whom Alexander was said to believe he was the son of, and which was apparently later confirmed to him by the Oracle of Amun at Siwa), and numerous Greek inscriptions, among them one describing the extravagant transportation of the body to the tomb (perhaps written by Ptolemy but omitting names and specifics).

In 1995 the team felt confident enough to make an international announcement of the discovery, causing a great stir of excitement but also political tensions (it was during the break-up of Yugoslavia and the Greek government was wary of a region attempting to proclaim a 'Republic of Macedonia'). The reaction from the Greek Prime Minister was to send an advisor to the Egyptian government, requesting the revocation of Souvaltzi's permission to excavate any further!

Twenty-two years on, Liana Souvaltzi continues to fight for permission to continue her work; she is convinced the Macedonian King lies in the tomb she discovered but cannot reveal…

Meanwhile in Alexandria …

A team of French archaeologists under Franck Goddio, in conjunction with the Egyptian Supreme Council of Antiquities (Department of Underwater Archaeology), began mapping the remains in the eastern section of the harbour in 1992, identifying the palace of Cleopatra on the submerged island of Antirrhodos (a royal property throughout the Ptolemaic period from 305 – 30 BC).

Many pundits theorise that Alexander's tomb, along with Marc Antony and Cleopatra's, are beneath the choppy waters of the once famous Great Harbour of Alexandria.

What are you waiting for?

We know the history is there, and as always, we must decide what to believe. I hope we can trust Strabo at least, he seemed like a trustworthy kind of guy and for my money gives us the best information, especially from a time when Alexander's tomb location was actually seen and recorded.

Do the research, come up with our own theory and dust off your hat because Alexander is awaiting discovery, hiding from you in an ancient burial place. My money says you'll need to take diving gear, and with any luck you'll soon be in the old harbour of Alexandria ready to test the waters.

CHAPTER 3

Hunt for the Flor do Mar

S ome say the richest shipwreck never found, the fate of this Portuguese treasure ship is a mystery for the ages. Built in Lisbon in 1502, she was christened Flor do Mar, meaning Flower of the Sea and intended to be at the forefront of the Portuguese empire's naval conquests across the globe.

Flor do Mar - Francisco Rodriguez, ca. Sixteenth century.

The Flor was a giant in her day, measuring thirty-six metres long by eight metres wide, weighing 400 tonnes and sporting three masts; an impressive carrack style ship that would first be given to the command of Estavao de Gama (brother of Vasco de Gama – the first European to reach India by sea).

She set out from her home thirsty for adventures, participating in the second Portuguese expedition to India (1505), the conquest of Ormuz (1507), the battle of Diu (1509), the defeat of Goa (1510) and the sacking of Malacca (1511).

Due to her size, the big old flower was notoriously unseaworthy and would undergo regular repairs throughout her life. Despite this, and despite being well past her use-by-date in 1511, she was given one last shot at glory – she would be the flag ship for the conquest of the famously rich port city of Malacca.

Located a couple of hours' train ride south of the modern Malaysian capital of Kuala Lumpur, the city was known as the 'Venice of the East', such was her wealth. The Sultanate of Malacca had grown incredibly rich as a trading mecca for merchants from as far as Arabia and China, a place where the Islamic methods of commerce proved lucrative for all involved, as traders were spared the harsh taxes often demanded by European controlled ports.

In July of 1511 and under the command of 'The Great' Afonso de Albuquerque (Afonso had also earned the titles 'The Terrible' and 'The Caesar of the East' during his highly successful military career), the Flor do Mar and fleet were positioned at the harbour entrance to Malacca and demanded the Sultan's surrender.

Afonso de Albuquerque - Were his arms really that big?

Modern Malacca is a city of diverse cultures and histories, well worth a visit.

With an answer not forthcoming, and because they could (the advanced long-range European cannons were unmatched at the beginning of the sixteenth century), the Portuguese bombarded the beautiful Asian citadel for days before they attacked, laying waste and systematically looting all in their path.

The sultan managed to escape the sacking, but rumour has it he did not flee empty handed; the legends surrounding his personal treasures abound in the area, particularly regarding the haunted island of Pulau Nangka... but for now we are focused on the motherload that left with the Flor do Mar, some of her inventory of which was recorded in the following passage:

> 'Aboard these ships are the rich plunder of Malacca and young boys and girls and specially the most rich objects ever seen. The Governor intended to offer them to Dona Maria, the Queen, and to the King himself. She was carrying a four legs table on which the Queen of Malacca used to take her meals that was worth 80.000 Cruzados. Even the merchants of Malacca offered 300.000 Cruzados to get it only for its precious stones. She was also carrying four sitting lions made of gold with perfumes inside. They used to be in the chamber of the King of Malacca, their eyes, tongs, teeth and nails

were made of precious stones and their estimated value was 200.000 Cruzados...'

Furthermore, there was a reported eight tonnes of gold ingots and other golden objects, 'countless' chests of precious stones and pearls and a large tribute from the King of Siam intended to appease the Portuguese royals. Some estimates have placed the cargo of the Flor do Mar in the region of **$3 billion USD**, making it possibly *the* most valuable treasure awaiting discovery.

With the city in ruins and the fleet full of spoils, the overloaded Flor do Mar and her friends charted a course for home and glory. Their arrival in Lisbon was to be the crowning achievement of every sailor and soldier and cook and captain among that proud and marauding Portuguese fleet (take a breath).

The fleet set sail, but it could not have been long before those on board must have felt the unease of a huge storm brewing on the horizon. During the night of the 20th of November 1511, and amidst a tempest likely prayed for by the survivors of the Malaccan siege, the Flor do Mar ran aground, the force of which split her wary body in two, somewhere off the north-east coast of the island of Sumatra, Indonesia. It was reported that 400 souls lost their lives aboard the Flor do Mar that night and, miraculously, Afonso de Albuquerque was rescued with five others via a lifeboat sent from the accompanying ship *Trinity*.

Ships in Distress in a Storm - Peter Monamy ca.1720.

The following uncredited eye witness account provides the most detail of the unfortunate events that fateful night:

'After the spoils, the Portuguese fleet set sail for Goa under the command of Afonso de Albuquerque with four other ships and a junk. The weather was fine with a calm sea when suddenly, sailing during the night along the coast of Sumatra, the fleet was hit by a terrible typhoon with huge waves and thunder. Trying to find refuge on the coast, the old and glorious Capitan was shipwrecked on the beach. Her old and rotten body opened itself and the ship was cut in two pieces. Her back completely embedded in the sand was demolished by the waves.

On the deck, Albuquerque tried to protect the daughter of one of his slaves waiting for their death. In this terrible situation, the jolly boat of the closest ship, the Trinity, succeeded in saving the Admiral as well as several other Portuguese, five in total. But the ship was fatally lost with her rich cargo and more than 400 men... With the Flor do Mar was lost the treasure for the King, gold, jewels and precious stones. Amongst the personal effects of the Governor were two lions in brass and the famous magic bracelet of the Rajah of Sabandar.'

And this excerpt from Portuguese chronicler Joao de Barros, describing the events after the Flor do Mar sailed from Malacca:

> *'Above all they had to brave the fury of the storms at sea and the danger of the sandbanks near the coasts ... The truth of this we are going to see in the notable example of Afonso de Albuquerque, who left Malacca with his galleons filled with trophies, sailed as far as the Kingdom of Aru to the end of the region called Timia in Sumatra. There at night his galleon was dashed against a hidden reef and broke up into two parts with the poop in one section and the prow in the other, because the ship was old and the seas heavy.'*

Further contemporary accounts have provided the following clues essential to our search:

- *Sunk in four fathoms of water (seven metres)*
- *Within cannon shot of the shore*
- *Just opposite the Kingdom of Daru*
- *Some survivors reached the River Pacem*

It should be noted that the geography of the Sumatran coastline has changed a lot during the past 500 years. Besides the fact that records and anecdotal evidence from the era are notoriously unreliable, the area in question is subject to high currents and extremely low visibility. You will need to calculate the changing coastal features, for example, has the shore receded or advanced on the sea? I don't know about you but I think this is nature doing her bit to guard this secret, and it's just a bonus because it means she hasn't been found yet ...

Many have said that locals would surely have salvaged many of the treasures once the storm cleared, but what of the unique inventory that still has not surfaced in any historical record since? Items such as the priceless golden lions that had been a gift from the Emperor of China to the Sultan of Malacca. Not to mention countless chests of gold and jewels that would have been impossible to fence or secrete into the local economy.

A Few Have Tried - Now It's Your Turn

Based on eyewitness accounts such as those you have just read; many searches have been conducted over the years. These include attempts by the South East Asian Salvage Company (SEAS). In 1989 this well-resourced conglomerate used the reports of survivors having reached the River Pacem as a start, setting up survey points between Timiang and Pasai (approx. ninety kilometres apart). The search was uneventful until an archaeologist claimed to know the location of the wreck near Karang Timau... a large magnetometer reading was discovered 200 metres southwest of Tengah Reef and excitement would have peaked amongst the treasure hunters. Alas, divers cleared away the sand and found... nothing. The search was abandoned in 1992.

Former Indonesian President Soeharto is reported to have spent over $20,000,000 searching for the wreck, a modest investment if he had been successful.

I have trekked along the tropical Sumatran coast between the River Pacem and Pasai, and plan on returning to hunt for any signs of the Flor do Mar. The Indonesian government will currently go fifty-fifty on any finds, not a bad split for $1.5 billion.

Hire a boat with a few mates out of Medan, or catch a taxi to the Sumatran coast and start walking with your metal detector. Either way, get involved because the reward is ridiculous. Otherwise ... Stay at home and read about it when another 'amateur treasure hunter' makes history.

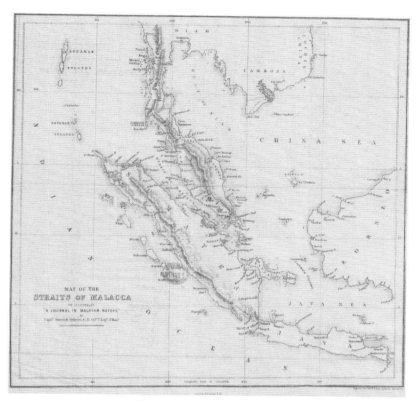

The Strait of Malacca, Ca. 1860

CHAPTER 4

The Fenn Treasure

I love this story. As far as 'treasure' goes, it's so recent and the individual behind it so intriguing that one can't help but be drawn to it.

In a gold-plated nutshell, there is a wealthy antiquities and arts dealer from Santa Fe, New Mexico, his name is Forrest Fenn and he wants you to be rich. When Forrest thought he was going to die of cancer in 1988, he decided to fill a treasure chest with over a million dollars in gold, jewellery, gems, rare coins and valuable artefacts (and a copy of his biography in an olive jar). He planned to bury the treasure somewhere in the Rocky Mountains and thereby make it his legacy; a way to ignite the adventurer within others and a prize for those worthy of its discovery.

Forrest didn't die. In fact, he courageously fought off cancer and is still alive today. Not to worry though, after years of the chest collecting dust in his attic, and at the ripe age of 80 years, Forrest decided to drive into the Rockies around 2010, go for a wander and bury the chest in his secret location after all. Estimated value today? - **$5 Million US Dollars.**

What's in the chest?

The chest itself is a Romanesque bronze lock box dated to around 1150 AD, and contains:

- Gold coins (mostly American Eagles and Double Eagles)

- Gold placer nuggets from Alaska (two weigh more than a pound each and there are hundreds of smaller ones)
- Pre-Columbian gold animal figures
- Ancient Chinese human faces carved from jade
- A 17th Century Spanish gold ring
- A large emerald once found with a metal detector
- An antique ladies' gold dragon coat bracelet that contains 254 rubies, six emeralds, two Ceylon sapphires and numerous small diamonds
- A Tairona and Sinu Indian necklace from Columbia that contains quartz crystal, carnelian, jadeite and other exotic stones
- A cast gold jaguar claw and a frog made of the same

Gold American Double Eagles, 1849.

Artist's Impression of you after finding Fenn's Treasure.

The Clues

In a subsequent memoir titled *Thrill of the Chase*, Fenn made the treasure hunt public knowledge and included a twenty-four-line poem. This crafty poem contains nine hidden clues that, if solved, will supposedly lead the master of the riddle to the treasure's hiding place. Before reading the poem however, here are a few of the clues leaked out by Fenn to searchers over the past seven years:

- *At least 8.25 miles north of Santa Fe, New Mexico*

- *More than 300 miles west of Toledo*

- *Located above 5,000 ft. and below 10,200 ft.*

- *In an area with pine trees*

- *Not in a graveyard, mine, or other man-made structure*

- *Not in close proximity to a human trail*

- *Not in a place an eighty-year-old man could not go*

- *The treasure is exposed to rain and snow, and could be scorched in a fire*

- *Searchers have come within 500 feet of the treasure*

- *It is not in Idaho or Utah*

The Rocky Mountains extend south from Canada through the US states of Idaho, Montana, Wyoming, Utah and New Mexico... We can already rule out two of these as per Fenn's statements, and once you get the altitude range in an area with pines trees... You are half way there already.

Black Bears, Grizzlies and Grey Wolves will likely be encountered on this quest – Avoid.

The Poem

As I have gone alone in there
And with my treasures bold
I can keep my secret where
And hint of riches new and old

Begin it where warm waters halt
And take it in the canyon down
Not far, but too far to walk
Put in below the home of Brown

From there it's no place for the meek
The end is ever drawing nigh
There'll be no paddle up your creek
Just heavy loads and water high

If you've been wise and found the blaze
Look quickly down, your quest to cease
But tarry scant with marvel gaze,
Just take the chest and go in peace.

So why is it that I must go,
And leave my trove for all to seek?
The answers I already know,
I've done it tired, and now I'm weak.

So hear me all and listen good,
Your effort will be worth the cold.
If you are brave and in the wood,
I give you title to the gold.

Where are the nine clues hidden in the poem?

The following theories have been harvested for you from the twenty-four-lines of Fenn's riddle:

As I have gone alone in there,
A gap or hole big enough for only one person? A cave perhaps?

*And with my treasures **bold**,*
'Bold' in Old English is 'Bald' – there is a Bald Mountain next to Jardine, Montana, which is right up from the Black 'Canyon' of the Yellowstone, which is where Joe 'Brown' discovered gold in Bear Creek.

There is also another Bald Mountain next to Kirwin, Wyoming. On the other side of Kirwin there is also 'Brown' Mountain, and the river running through Kirwin is 'Wood' River.

*I can keep my **secret** where,*
Secret Valley – just north of the Madison River in Yellowstone and only ten miles from where Forrest grew up.

Ojo Caliente – the last hot spring on the Firehole heading north in Yellowstone. Forrest mentions in his blog how he liked to swim where the hot spring waters mixed with the cool river water… Where warm waters halt?

*And **hint** of **riches new and old**,*
The origin of the word 'hint' is from 'hunt'.

Riches new and old could be a reference to an Indian cave (old) containing the chest (new).

***Begin** it where **warm waters halt**,*
A place where the water becomes colder (or hotter).

This is the only couplet in the poem that doesn't rhyme – given that it reportedly took fifteen years to compose, maybe 'halt' has some added significance?

Fenn has stated this does not refer to a dam.

*And take it **in the canyon down**,*

The water runs down into a canyon… Seems to easy.

*Not far, but **too far to walk**,*

The title of Fenn's second book on the treasure. Car or boat required maybe?

I'd say a boat…

Put in below the home of Brown.

"Brown" is capitalised – a reference to a person or landmark?

'Put-in' – put your boat in below the home of Brown… Brown Bear? There are only Black Bears known to live in the Rocky Mountains, however their fur can often be dark brown or cinnamon coloured. Perhaps a bear nicknamed by Forrest during his youth that made its home in the area?

Was the treasure 'Put-in' the water below the home of Brown?

Brown Mountain Campground is on the 'Wood' River south-east of Meeteetse (possibly the end of warm waters).

Brown House is at the bottom of Brown's Hill Road, near the banks of the Little Snake River, Wyoming, and there is a cemetery upstream ('end is drawing nigh').

Forrest has said that if you knew the House of Brown, you could walk right to the treasure.

*From there it's **no place for the meek**,*

This is lengthy but... Almost 200 years ago, near Devil's Slide at the base of Cinnabar Mountain, Montana, Joseph Meek and his companions were attacked by Indians and he was separated, wandering off into what is now Yellowstone and discovering Mammoth Hot Springs. This is right alongside Yellowstone River, down a canyon after the last of the hot springs. Furthermore, Joe Brown's 'Put-in' is not far downstream, on the other side of the water. Right on top of Cinnabar Mountain is the ghost-town and cemetery of Aldridge ('no place for the meek', 'the end is nigh'). Just upstream is another abandoned town called Electric. Electric, Montana, used to provide the electricity to all the local mines ('heavy loads').

*The end is ever drawing **nigh**;*
Old usage of the word 'nigh' meant 'left'.

*There'll be **no paddle up your creek**,*
The creek/ river flow is strong... or maybe it's a dry creek bed? No paddle needed or just too hard to paddle?

*Just **heavy loads and water high**.*
A waterfall?
Reportedly, the chest and contents weigh around twenty kilograms...
'Queen's Laundry' is located right by Ojo Caliente and the Firehole.

*If you've been wise and found the **blaze**,*
Forrest has said 'the blaze' refers to a specific object that wouldn't be feasible for someone to move. Apparently, Forrest has intimated that once you find 'the blaze', you'd almost certainly be able to see the chest, you could miss it – but you probably wouldn't.
A trail-blaze is often a mark on a tree or similar.

Bunsen Peak in Yellowstone is near the Mammoth Hot Springs and just down the canyon from it.

Look quickly down, your quest to cease,
But *tarry scant with marvel gaze*,
Reference to an amazing view?

This line literally means you shouldn't hang about to enjoy the view... But why not? Some think it's because the chest is in the water and you'll float right past it if you're not quick enough.

What about a cave full of sleeping bears who are escaping the 'cold' mentioned below?

*Just take the chest and **go in peace**.*

Go in peace so you don't wake the bears who are hibernating in a cave; the home of Brown.

So why is it that I must go,
And leave my trove for all to seek?
The answers I already know,
I've done it tired, and now I'm weak.
*So **hear me all** and **listen good**,*

'Listen good' is terrible English... Should be 'Listen well'... meaning it is either an important term or included just to rhyme with 'wood', which would make 'wood' a significant part of the poem.

Ear Spring is near Old Faithful and Solitary Geyser in Yellowstone.

Amphitheatre Lake is just down from Lake Solitude (alone) in Grand Teton National Park, Wyoming.

*Your effort will be worth the **cold**.*

Do you need to get wet? Maybe underwater?

A bear cave you can only enter in the winter while they are sleeping?

*If you are **brave** and **in the wood**,*

Fenn has stated the treasure is in proximity to pine trees; an area designated as 'woods' containing pine would be convenient.

Possibly inside a wooden object, a hollowed tree or beaver dam…

Many theories have the location of the treasure close to Wood River, while others are convinced that she lies in Lake of the Woods, North Yellowstone, just south of Mammoth Hot Springs and close to Indian Creek ('brave'). Lake of the Woods is nowadays not so popular due to a lack of fish, but it was full of trout when Fenn was young and frequented the area.

I give you title to the gold.

The original last line to the poem was 'Just take the chest and leave my bones', implying that Fenn meant to die alongside the treasure (obviously he didn't). If this is the meaning, then the location must be somewhere a human could fit, and somewhere a body would remain undisturbed by wolves and scavengers. Also, the word 'chest' appears in line sixteen, so this must have been moved there from the last line as it was too important to leave out.

But Which Clues??

There are as many potential clues as your imagination will allow. However, as mentioned, there are only nine in the poem, and Fenn has strongly hinted that the first is contained within the line:

'Begin it where warm waters halt'.

Jump online because there are numerous sites, blogs and Facebook groups dedicated to this cause that will keep you entertained (or confused) for days on end. That is probably the best thing about this treasure, so many people have already put in the hard yards for you!

You have help not only from Fenn himself, who is hit with daily enquiries from an estimated more than 350,000 searchers over the past nine years (this has also included death threats, bribes, and people constantly arriving to his house uninvited and causing enough hassle for 911 to have been called three times), but also from precisely those same treasure hunters who have braved the wilderness and come up empty. Consider it your own vast personal pool of theories and failures leading you ever closer to the location of the chest.

A scene from the vast Yellowstone National Park – a location central to most searches (and a hell of a camping trip).

Go Prepared...

As of the end of 2017, three people have died while searching the wilderness for the Fenn Treasure. It's always best to go with friends, inform the local authorities of your plans, and ensure you take adequate supplies (including a GPS, plenty of water and bear mace - really). Also, don't bother packing your metal detector or shovel if you are looking within Yellowstone – both detecting and digging are illegal in the park, and Fenn has stated the treasure is not buried underground. Happy hunting!

CHAPTER 5

The Real Treasure Island

Duration the era of piracy in the New World, there were no banks or safety deposits for pirates to store their loot. This meant that secret, off the map locations became the only way for these marauders of the sea to safeguard their ill-gotten gains.

There is an island in the Caribbean, a small paradise 550 km south west from Costa Rica known as Cocos Island; she is famous in fiction and truth as the home of pirate treasure. Measuring less than twenty-four square kilometres and covered in lush green wildlife, Jacques Cousteau credited her as the most beautiful place on earth, she was the inspiration behind Robert Louis Stevenson's *Treasure Island* and also for Michael Crichton's monumental *Jurassic Park*. Both legend and reason tell us that Cocos Island is home to more than one splendid bounty.

Picturesque Cocos Island from the air.

Picturesque Cocos Island from the ground.

The Treasure of Lima

The tales of treasure for this Pacific gem are mouth-watering and there are several; let's begin with the legendary *Treasure of Lima*. The year was 1820 and revolution was afoot in Peru. Along with neighbouring countries also caught up in the fervour of independence, rebels started a war with the colonial Spanish empire. Argentine General Jose de San Martin promptly planned an invasion of Lima, the Peruvian capital. Jose de la Serna, the Spanish Viceroy to Lima, decided it would be a good idea to safeguard the church's wealth in one location; at least until the local hell raisers had calmed down. Word was sent to the fifty odd churches in the area to deliver all their valuables to the Port of Callao.

The combined value of all that ecclesiastical gold and glitter?

An astonishing **$208,000,000** in today's currency. In addition to tonnes of gold and silver, the official inventory, included:

1 chest of gold trimmings of altar cloth with baldachins, monstrance and chalices coated with up to 1,244 gem stones

1 chest containing 2 gold reliquaries weighing 54 Kg with 636 topazes, cornelians, emeralds and diamond gemstones

1 chest containing 3 reliquaries of cast metal weighing 72.5 Kg with 869 rubies, 19 diamonds and other gem stones

1 chest containing 4,000 doubloons of Spanish pieces of eight, 124 swords, 5,000 crowns on Mexican gold, 64 dirks, 120 shoulder belts and 28 rondaches

1 chest containing 8 caskets of cedar wood and silver with 3,840 cut precious stones, rings, patens and an additional 4,265 uncut precious stones

A 7-foot solid gold statue of the Virgin Mary weighing 354 Kg, adorned with 1,684 gem stones including 4-inch emeralds, 6-inch topazes and 7 crosses made of diamonds

7 chests containing 22 candelabras of gold and silver weighing 113 Kg and with 164 rubies

The Viceroy soon grew wary of Callao's security, however, and planned to put the enormous treasure into the hold of a ship and send her to Mexico – at least until the Spaniards had contained the situation on-shore. Who would you trust with such an audacious task and with such a prize? A British Captain no less! That's right, Captain William Thompson, a 'trusted' trader and the man at the helm of the ship *Mary Dear*, was chosen by the Spanish to fulfil the mission. Captain Thompson piously saw to the loading of a priceless treasure aboard his vessel. The *Mary Dear* set sail for the open sea with a small crew, as well as six Spanish soldiers and two priests who were to guard the treasure at all times.

Who knows when the temptation became too much for Captain Thompson, or if he had planned it all along, but at some point, he decided on a course of action that would brand him forevermore as a pirate. The eight Spanish defenders of the Treasure of Lima had their throats cut while they slept, then they were thrown to the sharks during a single bloody night aboard the *Mary Dear*. Captain Thompson set a course for Cocos Island where he and his men buried the *Treasure of Lima*, agreeing to part ways and lay low until it would be safe to recover the loot.

Captain Thompson's not so well thought out plan soon unravelled, however, as a roaming Spanish warship intercepted the *Mary Dear*, soon realising she was lighter than when she left port; to the tune of one treasure, six soldiers and two priests to be precise. Captain and crew were placed on trial for the dreaded crime of Piracy, convicted and promptly executed... except for Captain Thompson and his lucky First-Mate. Logic dictated the Spaniards would need a guide to recover their riches, or at least that's how the silver-tongued sailors must have sold the idea.

The not-so-trustworthy Captain William Thompson.

The inept Spanish authority, already having made terrible errors in judgement, were then left for idiotas on the beach of Cocos Island, as Captain Thompson and his first mate somehow managed to get the slip on their armed guards and abscond into the thick jungle. Amazingly, the Spanish were unable to find the crafty couple and eventually marooned them there.

Once the coast was clear (literally) and the pair had finished counting their lucky stars, they secreted what treasure they could carry on themselves, then managed to draw the attention of a whaling vessel; hitching a ride to what is now known as Puntas Arenas in Costa Rica. Unfortunately, the unnamed first mate had his luck run out at this point in the story, succumbing to Yellow Fever and leaving a sole survivor with the known whereabouts of the *Treasure of Lima*.

So, it was down to Captain William Thompson of the Scottish merchant navy, lately a pirate and the last man alive with a priceless secret. However, perhaps weary of his luck also running out, he disappeared from history without a trace after having landed in Puntas Arenas... Until his death in 1841. Like a page straight out of *Treasure Island* or *The Count of Monte Cristo*, Captain Thompson decided, on his death bed and sensing his last, to divulge his great secret to a good friend, John Keating. Various versions of Captain Thompson's instructions have surfaced over the years, including:

> *'Once there follow the coast line of the bay until you find a creek, where, at high water mark, you go up the bed of a stream which flows inland. Now you step seventy paces, west by south, and against the skyline you will see a gap in the hills. From any other point, the gap is invisible. Turn north and walk to a stream. You will see now a rock with a smooth face, rising sheer like a cliff. At the height of a man's shoulder, above the ground, you will see a hole large enough for you to insert your thumb. Thrust in an iron bar, twist it round in the cavity, and behind you will find a door which opens on the treasure.'*

And this version, reportedly also from Captain Thompson on his deathbed:

> *'Disembark in the Bay of Hope between two islets, in water five fathoms deep. Walk three hundred and fifty paces along the course of the stream then turn north-northeast for eight hundred and fifty yards, stake, the setting sun*

stake draws the silhouette of an eagle with wings spread. At the extremity of sun and shadow, cave marked with a cross. There lies the treasure.'

Behaving like any self-respecting middle-aged man, Keating immediately arranged a treasure hunt to Cocos Island. Keating anchored in Chatham Bay, he and the ship's Captain (Bogue) going alone ashore. After a time, Keating and Captain Bogue returned empty-handed to the anxious and expectant crew. Not believing a word of their uneventful expedition, the crew thought the two had concealed the treasure's location and were not wanting to share. The crew insisted on a more thorough search of the island.

You can imagine the awkward exchange between the crew with Captain Bogue and Keating, until eventually, the crew would not be taken for fools; tempers boiled over and the two untrusted leaders were forced to abandon ship! They frantically swam to shore, hiding amidst the jungle like their predecessors, and once again managing to evade capture. There is no doubt the crew would have searched for the treasure, but there is also no doubt that Keating would not have given up the location easily, making for a frantic game of cat and mouse until the crew decided they would make do with the ship, marooning Keating and Bogue in a scene reminiscent of Captain Thompson and his first mate all those years before.

'Bahia Chatham' or 'Chatham Bay' in the North East corner of the map.

Months later, an unsuspecting ship anchored in Chatham Bay to replenish her freshwater supply. Keating met the landing party and told them he was the sole survivor of a shipwreck. Keating later amended his account to say Captain Bogue had drowned in a stream on the island... Original.

Keating made it back to the mainland and, using the small amount of riches he had managed to smuggle, organised two more expeditions to the island. However, either having lost his bearings or unwilling to split the treasure again, Keating was only able to cover his expenses. There are holes in this account I know; in the end Keating was broke and broken, I imagine much to the entertainment of local tavern visitors as he told drunken tales of the incredible *Treasure of Lima* buried on Cocos Island.

Unwilling to die with the secret, Keating left instructions with a Quartermaster by the name of Nicholas Fitzgerald. Fitzgerald never raised the money to launch an expedition to Cocos Island, but left the details from Keating in the form of a letter, now preserved at the Nautical and Traveller's Club in Sydney, Australia. Registered under No. 18, 755, it may not make a lot of sense until you study the lay out of the island (hint - Google Earth), but nonetheless reads:

> *'At two cables lengths, south of the last watering-place, on three points. The cave is the one which is to be found under the second point. Christie, Ned and Anton have tried but none of the three has returned. Ned on his fourth dive found the entrance at twelve fathoms but did not emerge from his fifth dive. There are no octopuses but there are sharks. A path must be opened up to the cave from the west. I believe there has been a rock fall at the entrance.'*

Two further sources also stated the following descriptions worth a look:

> *'The hiding place has been calculated to be within 100 yards of 5 degrees, 30 minutes, 17 seconds latitude north and 87 degrees, 0 minutes, 40 seconds longitude west, south of the Bay of Hope, north-northeast of Muele Island, possibly in a cave that is accessible at low tide.'*

> *'Buried in four caches within 100 yards of each other, in an area an eighth of a mile inland near Chatham Bay.'*

The Devonshire Treasure

There is supposedly a treasure on Cocos Island that predates the *Treasure of Lima*, and by all accounts may be larger. The story begins in the year 1818 and centres on another British naval officer, this time one Captain Bennett Grahame. Captain Grahame commanded the very English-sounding survey vessel, *HMS Devonshire,* and was tasked with surveying the coast from Cape Horn to Panama. However, he grew bored of the lowly paid public service and, seeing an enormous opportunity, convinced his fellow officers and crew to turn to a life of piracy. It is said the men were given the option of turning pirate or being put ashore in Panama, only the honest crew never made it that far and were allegedly put to death on Cocos Island – an ideal pirate hideout with fresh water, a vast network of caves and located far from the main shipping routes, though still close enough to plunder the Pacific coast.

During the ensuing years, Captain Grahame amassed over 350 tonnes of gold from Spanish treasure galleons he raided in the Pacific. If you do the calculations... that's over **$2.25 billion dollars** in today's currency – no wonder the crew turned pirate when the naval conditions were harsh and the salary worse.

Unfortunately for Captain Grahame and his crew, they were unable to enjoy the spoils of their venture as they were nearly all arrested and executed before they had the chance. There is a twist in the tale of the *HMS Devonshire*, however, for she had aboard a female crew member named Mary Welch (almost a Wench). Perhaps because she was a woman, she was spared the executioner; instead she was sent to a penal colony and later released.

What did Mary do as soon as she was free? She went after the gold she had witnessed Captain Grahame bury on Cocos Island of course! Armed with charts, navigation equipment and bearings, she was sure she would be able to find the exact location of the Spanish gold. Welch led the expedition – only to find the landmarks she had committed to memory all those years ago were no longer there... The expedition failed and the Spanish gold remained at slumber.

The real treasures of Cocos Island – The renowned adventurer Jacques Cousteau called it the most beautiful place on earth.

Benito Bonito Goes Cocos

Benito Bonito was a shadowy figure, said to be a very successful Portuguese pirate of the Pacific circa 1818. Given that no solid records exist of his birth, his capture or his execution, there is an alternative explanation – Benito Bonito and Captain Bennett Grahame were one and the same person.

The nickname given to Bonito, that of 'Bloody Sword', is in fact the moniker earned by Captain Grahame as he put to death all those who would not join him upon turning pirate in 1818 (also the year we begin to hear of Bonito's exploits in the exact same area). Adopting a Portuguese persona would have would have helped to curtail the English navy's interest in Grahame, at least for a while.

Benito 'Bloody Sword' Bonito.

Bonito amassed a fortune plundering the rich Spanish treasure ships transporting South America's stolen wealth. In 1819, he hit the jackpot when seizing a rich mule train from near Acapulco. He had the plunder loaded aboard his vessel and sailed straight for Cocos Island. Then the treasure was:

> *'Stashed in caves under a projecting tongue of land on the north side of Wafer's Bay'.*

It's also reported that after a successful attack on five Spanish galleons, Bonito again headed to his favourite island, where he had a thirty-five-foot tunnel constructed to hide the loot.

Bonito's luck ran out when he was cornered by a British war ship in the Bay of Buena Ventura; his ship was sunk and he, along with most of his crew, were taken to England and hanged for piracy. Funnily enough, those spared the noose where sent to the penal settlement in Tasmania, Australia, including a certain young woman named Mary Welch who also claimed Benito was none other than the esteemed Captain Bennett Grahame, formally of the British Navy.

Edward Davis

Edward Davis was an English privateer operating in the Caribbean during the 1680s, much earlier than our other associations to Cocos Island, and maybe the first example of the island being used as a treasure bank. Davis sailed under various buccaneers and privateers and made the acquaintance of renowned explorer and writer William Dampier; his exploits were recorded in Dampier's *A New Voyage Round the World*.

In 1684 and while privateering aboard the captured *Bachelor's Delight* under Captain John Cook, Davis found himself with a promotion, the crew electing him to lead after Cook's death. Numerous raids on the Pacific coast and seizures from Spanish silver fleets made Davis a rich man, although by 1688 he had run afoul of the authority; he was arrested for piracy and tried in Virginia. It seems a grey area for some in either the privateering (plundering enemy ship's in your country's name, usually with written permission) or the piracy game; the former was condoned by King James in a 1685 Proclamation and appears to be the excuse by which Davis escaped the hangman. However, in 1690 he was ordered back to England (without his possessions); the *Bachelor's Delight* was sold to continue her adventures elsewhere.

As for Cocos Island, reports indicate that Davis anchored in Chatham Bay and then buried two caches; one of several chests containing ingots, Spanish pieces-of-eight and 140 tonnes of silver bar and plate, and the other of 733 bars of gold, seven kegs of gold coin and a quantity of church jewels and ornaments.

This kind of stopover and bury your loot scenario must have been common in the age of piracy, and fits well with the fact that Davis returned to England empty-handed.

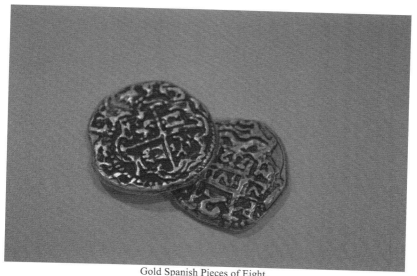

Gold Spanish Pieces of Eight.

Search Attempts Thus Far

Every man and his dog, from President Franklin D. Roosevelt to famous Australian actor Errol Flynn (who played a 17th century pirate in a film titled *Captain Blood)*, has had a shot at finding treasure on Cocos Island. The hundreds of expeditions launched over the years have turned up mixed results, some of which have included:

1845 - A British explorer claims to have found a chest of Spanish gold coins in a cave overlooking Wafer Bay.

1856 - Treasure was said to be uncovered on the island by a group of mercenaries escaping from Nicaragua. It is reportedly written that one of the mercenaries pulled on a bronze chain that was found in a sea cave and it led to a chest full of Spanish doubloons.

1880 - An expedition by a group of soldiers was said to have been successful in the vicinity of Wafer Bay. A 'small excavation in the face of the cliff' apparently held a large amount of English and French coins together with a pile of 300 silver ingots.

1889 - Prussian adventurer August Gissler lived on the island from 1889 to 1908, however only managed to uncover 6 gold coins.

1931 - A Belgian hunter reportedly found a two-foot gold Madonna statue.

1939 - A single bar of gold was found in a small stream near a waterfall.

2012 – Reports that local park Rangers found $200,000,000 in gold while assessing a hurricane event... this report has appeared multiple times in 'fake news' outlets and is thus far unsubstantiated.

Best Go and See for Yourself

Aside from the immense wealth already discussed, Cocos Island has further been associated with the English privateer Francis Drake, the pirate captains William Kidd and Henry Morgan, and even a persistent legend of Incan treasure near the summit of Mount Iglesias, the highest point on the island.

One problem may be that the shoreline has naturally shifted over the years, explaining why those who followed the bearings of Captain Thompson and Mary Welch, for example, only ended up digging in the wrong places. It is possible that many beaches and caves of the early 19th century are now well under the sea, all the better for us!

Fortunately for Cocos Island, she became a World Heritage Listed site in 1997, conservation efforts became the priority and treasure hunting as such has been banned since the 1970s. Any attempts or visits to the island would need written permission from the authorities to satisfy the local rangers who are now the guardians of paradise.

Most recently, an international team gained access to the island under a combined geological, archaeological and ecological mission. Well aware of the prospect of other 'fortuitous finds' during their ten-day stay on the island, the expedition leaders struck a deal with the Costa Rican government – any treasure discovered would be handed over to them, but only after a generous salvage fee had been agreed on.

I suppose if you are going to start hunting on Cocos Island, you need a little creativity (or secrecy) with regards to your reasons for being there in the first place. Buena Suerte!

CHAPTER 6

Yamashita's Gold

Treasure hunting in the Philippines is a national past time for those seeking a fast way to fortune. Whether it's hunting the caches of silver dollars left over from the Philippine-American War, the missing treasures of Francisco Dagohoy from the Spanish era, or the lost loot of the 16th century Chinese pirate Limahong, there has always been a legend to inspire the adventurer in anyone game enough. It's no surprise, then, that in seeking the reported 175 treasure hordes of Yamashita, the local populations are turning over every stone and exploring every likely cave in the pursuit of riches..

As the Japanese Empire advanced ruthlessly through Asia during the Second World War, not only did it conquer every country in its path, it took possession of thousands of years' worth of sovereign wealth. The nations we know as China, Korea, Thailand, Myanmar, Vietnam, Cambodia, the Philippines, Malaysia, Hong Kong, Singapore, Papua New Guinea, Timor and Indonesia were systematically occupied and stripped of their riches by the Japanese imperial forces, gaining much needed resources intended to finance the expensive war effort.

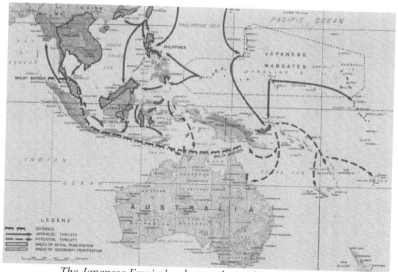

The Japanese Empire's advance during World War Two.

The looting of banks, religious buildings, private estates and museums meant an enormous cargo had been amassed towards the end of World War II, however the Japanese were unable to transport it home to Japan, as by this stage US naval forces had blocked their return to the homeland. It is at this point said that the princes of Emperor Hirohito's household, led by Prince Yasuhito Chichibu and Prince Takeda Tsuneyoshi, hatched a plan to safeguard the war loot. The tide of war had turned against them and, realising that it would be perilous for the wealth to fall into enemy hands, they mapped out 175 secret locations in which to divide and conceal the precious horde. Dubbed the *'Golden Lily'* organisation, the majority of the loot locations are said to be in the Philippines, hence the legend of *Yamashita's Gold*, named for the Japanese Commander of the Philippines at the time.

Astonishingly, estimates have placed the present-day combined value of the Yamashita hordes as somewhere between **$100 Billion and $1 Trillion US.**

General Tomoyuki Yamashita

In November of 1941, General Yamashita was given command of the Japanese 25th Army at the height of World War II. He immediately initiated an invasion of Malaya, his force of 30,000 troops relied on speed to capture Singapore against 80,000 British, Indian and Australian troops – it was the largest surrender of British-led personnel in history and earned him the nickname *The Tiger of Malaya*.

Yamashita assumed command of the Japanese forces in the Philippines in October of 1944; not an ideal post as 200,000 US troops landed near Manila in January of 1945. What was Yamashita's role to be this late in a losing war? Was his sole purpose to safeguard the immense war loot from enemy hands?

Isolated and after intense fighting and delaying tactics, Yamashita surrendered to the British General Arthur Percival on the 2nd of September 1945. Ironically, it was Percival who had surrendered Singapore to Yamashita in 1941.

Late in 1945, Yamashita was tried for war crimes relating to massacres in the Philippines and Singapore against civilians and prisoners. Many regarded these actions completely against the character and morality of Yamashita; he was known to disagree with the harsh orders of his superiors on several occasions, and would punish his own men if he heard of such war crimes in his ranks. Regardless, a precedent would be set in what became known as the 'Yamashita Standard' – this would ensure commanders accepted responsibility for their subordinate's actions, whether the actions of their men were known or not. On the 23rd of February 1946, Yamashita was hanged in a prison camp south of Manila.

Before his death, however, Yamashita is reported to have meticulously mapped the 175 treasure locations in an ancient coded form of Japanese writing. Known as Kanji, the maps would have looked illegible to a mono-linguist from, for example, the United States Army.

General Yamashita.

Prince Yasuhito Chichibu

Prince Chichibu was the leader of the so called 'Golden Lily' organisation. A military man but also an Oxford scholar, Chichibu was tasked with overseeing the redistribution of wealth from South-East Asia to the Japanese Empire. He died in 1953 of tuberculosis.

Prince Chichibu.

Prince Takedo Tsuneyoshi

Prince Takedo began his military career in 1930, assuming various roles, including apparently assisting in the designation of 175 treasure vaults throughout the Philippines. Eyewitnesses repeatedly allege Takedo's involvement, particularly towards the end of the war. A fun fact – he served on the International Olympic Committee from 1967 – 1981. He died in 1992 from natural causes.

Prince Tsuneyoshi.

Why the Philippines?

Initially the Golden Lily centred its operations and growing store of loot in Singapore, but towards the end of the war shifted to the Philippines in an attempt to transport treasures home from there. However, the US naval forces had become too dominant, preventing safe passage to Japan and reportedly sinking several treasure laden ships before the strategy of 'hide and retrieve later' became the only option.

Tunnel Eight

Said to be the final hiding place used, the creatively named 'Tunnel Eight' is reportedly in the mountains of Luzon, north of Manila, and has become the best known of the caches. It is thought that in this place, the engineers and soldiers loyal to Japan drank and sang upon the completion of their work; the war was ending, and they had just completed the last of 175 secret tunnel complexes to safeguard a valuable asset for their country. However, their service would demand the ultimate price as, having ensured dynamite charges had been set and the merry workers were inside, it is said that General Yamashita and Prince Takeda slipped out, detonating the charges and sealing their loyal subjects as a means of securing secrecy; the ultimate sacrifice for their flag.

A source of information regarding this night claims to have been a valet to the Japanese princes in charge of sealing the treasure sites. The Filipino valet, Ben Valmores, claims he was spared from Tunnel Eight that very night by the grace of his war time master, Prince Takedo Tsuneyoshi. It is reported that in 1998, Valmores was tested on the identity of Takedo in a 1930s photograph of the royal family, from which he immediately recognised the prince.

After the sealing of Tunnel Eight, Prince Takedo returned to Japan via submarine, and General Yamashita remained with his army, surrendering to allied forces a few months later.

Baguio City, Luzon, Philippines.

Rogelio 'Roger' Roxas

One man who succeeded in finding treasure in the Philippines was Rogelio 'Roger' Roxas, a former soldier and locksmith from the town of Baguio, north of Manila on the island of Luzon.

In May of 1970, acting on a map provided by the son of a former Japanese soldier, together with testimony from General Yamashita's war time interpreter (who had described contents including gold, silver and a golden Buddha), Roger had spent his life savings to hire a team of labourers and was ready to begin his search. He had even obtained a permit and identified the area near Baguio Hospital, likely in the vicinity of the location known as 'Tunnel Eight' mentioned above.

After two weeks of searching an area covered in twenty-five years of thick jungle growth, Roger and company discovered a small cave entrance, not far from the hospital once used by Yamashita as his headquarters. The cave became a tunnel, and one-hundred metres into the cave,

Roger and his men encountered a collapsed dead-end. Roger knew this was a good sign and the team immediately got to digging.

After four months of dirt, sweat and tears, the team finally broke through the collapsed section. Buried behind the entrance to the chamber, the men found bayonets, samurai swords, radios and the remains of Japanese soldiers in military uniform... but no gold. Instead, Roger and his men encountered a complex network of tunnels that would take another six months for the team to explore; still they found no gold. All the while Roger's life savings had dwindled and he reached the point that he could not afford to keep the men on any longer. In a final hail Mary attempt with his metal detector, he searched one last section of the tunnels and heard the shrill of the machine as he ran it past what appeared to be a solid wall. Hacking into the wall, Roger quickly realised it was thin and eagerly broke through to yet another chamber. Shining his torch into the chamber, what he saw would have left him breathless.

The light from his torch shined back at him from a golden statue of Buddha, finally his prayers had been answered. But that wasn't all - Roger estimates there were over a thousand stacked crates filled with gold bars – Mother of God.

Roger Roxas and the golden Buddha he discovered.

Roger knew he couldn't take all of the discovery with him, so he decided to reseal the chamber, but removed the golden buddha and a single crate of twenty-four gold bars. Using ropes and pulleys to move the Buddha (estimated to weigh about a tonne), it took the strength of ten men just to relocate the statue to Roger's home. It was worth it though; this would give him the means to return with more men and trucks to empty the rest of the chamber.

Enter President / Dictator Ferdinand Marcos

News had spread quickly of Roger's discovery. Unfortunately for him, it had also reached the ears of the most powerful and dishonest man in the Philippines – none other than President Ferdinand Marcos.

Marcos and his wife Imelda famously made a living out of ripping off the Philippines. Despite being convicted, imprisoned and then acquitted of murdering his father's political rival when he was just eighteen years old, in 1965 Marcos was 'democratically' elected to the Philippine's presidential office, running on the back of his *incredible* war record during WWII. He claimed to have been awarded 27 medals of honour from the Philippines and the United States, including a Distinguished Service Medal (pinned by General Macarthur himself) and a Purple Heart... Needless to say, Marcos' service record is... questionable.

Regardless, Marcos enjoyed power and was able to somehow secure an unprecedented second term in 1969, followed by a declaration of Martial Law in 1972 that would be the pretext for him to rule until the people rose up in 1986. Marcos and his wife Imelda (who famously left over 2,300 pairs of shoes behind when the family fled the Philippines), allegedly siphoned off around $10 billion of state funds during their reign.

Marcos was ruthless and if he wanted something, he tended to get it. Also, he had passed a law requiring all treasure hunters to obtain a permit, then report back with the exact location if they found anything... Okay, now the story has its villain, let's get back to the hero, Rogelio Roxas...

Ferdinand and Imelda Marcos.

A Dream Come True

Returning home from his discovery, Rogelio 'Roger' Roxas must have been over the moon. Presenting his wife and new born child with a price-less golden Buddha and crate of gold bars, I can't imagine how ecstatic they must have felt. As if he couldn't have any more good fortune, Roger stayed up late that night and studied the golden Buddha, its face serene and all-knowing. Feeling an urge to test the durability of the object, Roger gently manoeuvred the head and was amazed when it twisted off in his hands, revealing 'two handfuls' of uncut diamonds inside. I doubt our hero would have slept that night.

Knowing that the sooner he went back the better, Roger quickly sold seven of the gold bars, and had the buddha appraised by two potential buyers:

- *Kenneth Cheatham performed a test by drilling a small hole in one of the Buddha's arms; he estimated the find to be 'solid twenty-two carats gold'*

- *Luis Mendoza performed a test using nitric acid; he estimated the find to be 'more than twenty carats gold'*

Things were going very well – Roger would soon be ready to return to the tunnel and complete his mission.

Unbeknownst to Roger, the permit he had applied for in the municipality of Baguio, as per government requirements, had been processed by none other than the uncle of President Ferdinand Marcos. The President soon heard of the discovery and immediately initiated his deceit.

On the night of April the 5th, 1971, a group of armed men stormed into Roger's family home, holding him at gun point and robbing him of the Buddha and the gold. The men left as quickly as they had appeared in the night. Roger was left with nothing.

Not to be intimidated, Roger immediately reported the theft to the Police but to no avail – the Police were in the President's pocket. The media's loyalty was harder to buy; here was a country growing tired of being cheated. Within days the theft was making headlines across the country, associating Marcos as a common thief, all at a time when political pressure was mounting on the brazenly corrupt President. The story had gained significant momentum in the press; Roger needed to be silenced.

On April the 19th, Roger received a call from the Baguio City courthouse – *his* gold Buddha had been deposited by members of the military and was ready to be collected. Roger took one look at the Buddha present-ed to him and saw it was a lacklustre imitation. He tried to remove the head and it wouldn't budge; Marcos had attempted to sway him with a fake. Roger headed to the media once again and made more damaging headlines.

Breaking Point

On May the 18th, armed men in civilian clothing arrested Roger in neighbouring Cabanatuan City. Over the coming days, Roger was beaten, burned and electrocuted until, after finally reaching his breaking point, he signed a statement to say Marcos had nothing to do with the theft from his home. Much worse, however, was that his torturers forced him to reveal the location of the remaining gold bars.

The man was now broken but, rather than set him free, Marcos had Roger imprisoned while he emptied the vault that he had worked so hard to discover. After three years in prison without charge, Roger was eventu-ally freed in 1974. He had by now lost everything, not just gold but pre-cious years with his family. For fear of further pain, Roger went into hiding, but he did not disappear from history just yet, the name Rogelio Roxas would make one last, defiant appearance.

Roger's Day in Court (Almost)

From the relative safety of the United States, in March of 1988 and some seventeen years after he had Yamashita's Gold torn from his grasp, Roger Roxas filed a lawsuit against Ferdinand and Imelda Marcos, the former Philippine first family who were now living a lavish exile in Ha-waii. The following timeline marks important events surrounding the legal battle:

In September 1989 in Honolulu, Ferdinand Marcos died of natural causes at the age of seventy-two.

In May 1993 in the Philippines, on the eve of court proceedings against Marcos, Rogelio 'Roger' Roxas died of unknown causes at the age of 49. The lawsuit was continued by Roger's family and the 'Golden Buddha Corporation' that was formed in his name.

In 1996, based largely on Roger's detailed testimony, a jury in Honolulu awarded $40 billion in compensatory damages to Roger's estate.

In 1998, however, the Hawaii Supreme Court reversed the judgment against Ferdinand and Imelda Marcos, citing insufficient evidence that Roger had found such a large amount of gold, existing only in 'unopened boxes' as per the testimony. The court instead awarded Roger's estate the value of the golden Buddha and the seventeen gold bars that Roger had removed from the find and not yet sold (stolen by Marcos' men). The court found the following:

- *'There was sufficient evidence to support the jury's special finding that Marcos converted the treasure that Roxas found.'*

- *'There was sufficient evidence to support the jury's determination that Roxas 'found' the treasure pursuant to Philippine law.'*

A lawyer for Roxas' estate currently has a $6 million judgement against Imelda Marcos for human rights abuses relating to Roger's imprisonment and torture.

Despite the verdicts in Roxas' favour, the likelihood of any money changing hands is slim to none. A lawyer for the Marcos family has remarked:

'It's Monopoly money. Everything in the Marcos estate is tied up by the Philippine government.'

Moving past the bureaucracy of the legal system to the present day, and thanks to Roger's son Henry Roxas, it is possible to visit the life story of our unfortunate hero. In the area of Lourdes Grotto in Baguio City, Henry will delight you with the 'true' story of his father's brilliant discoveries, then show you a replica of the famed golden Buddha, along with other relics and other war time artefacts uncovered by his late father.

Speaking in 1992, Imelda Marcos admitted that the Marcos' enormous wealth had been due to Yamashita's Gold, but it would be 'embarrassing' to admit it due to the value, which she estimated at ***$1 trillion***.

The US Connection

Though it seems a widely known fact that the Japanese forces conducted murder, plunder and looting on a massive scale throughout the years preceding and during World War II (see *'The Rape of Nanking'* for perhaps the worst example), there appears no mention of it in the initial post-war fall out. Indeed, the Imperial household goes unscathed throughout the trials for war crimes, and reparations are a footnote in the US led prosecution. If one is to compare the damages paid by the German nation to victims of WWII, and which are still being paid, they are a fraction of that which the 'bankrupt' Japan was made to pay. Some estimates have the difference at around $50 billion from Germany to Japan's $3 billion. This is despite the post-war boom in Japan that quickly saw the Pacific nation become an economic powerhouse and perpetual ally to the United States. To highlight the leniency offered to Japan's war time culprits, look at Nobusuke Kishi; although found guilty of war crimes, he would later become the Japanese Prime Minister in the 1950s.

There are some, including Sterling and Peggy Seagrave in their book 'Gold Wars', who argue that this is no coincidence. They assert that US intelligence were well aware of the Japanese war loot, having tracked their movements via undercover operatives throughout the course of the war. As Asian gold was largely unaccounted for on the international market, it was an ideal injection of wealth and its origins would be nigh untraceable.

The Seagraves claim a Captain Edward Lansdale of the OSS (Office of Strategic Services), along with a Filipino torture specialist named Santa Romana, were able to secure the whereabouts of twelve treasure locations from Yamashita's personal driver. The driver was able to show Lansdale and Romana these secret locations north of Manila, apparently filled with gold bars, tonnes of platinum, jars of diamonds and jewels, *more* golden artefacts and also several pieces of priceless artwork. Lansdale reported to General Macarthur, who in turn reported to US President Truman, and the decision was made to keep the discoveries a secret. The reasons were two-fold; such wealth could not be allowed to fall into enemy hands, and such a large amount of gold (if it were to enter the market) would cause economies pegged to the precious metal to crash, leading to economic calamity. The US allegedly deposited many billions worth into 170 banks across the world, then used them as a sort of Cold War piggy bank to further US interests around the world.

The US were also in need of an ally in a geo-political region dominated by the rise of Communism; Japan could provide this. Furthermore, military intelligence operatives have been named as colluding with the Japanese government to recover the Asian treasures, an enormous 'off the books' war chest that would serve to finance covert aspects of the Cold War and satisfy at least one nation's lust for post-war reparations. Coincidentally, in the modern day, the US budget for 'black operations' is estimated in the area of $50 billion a year, more than the reported Defence budgets of the United Kingdom and France combined. But that's enough of the conspiracy theories.

Wasn't Ghere 175 Vaults?

Presuming Roger's find was among the last concealed by General Yamashita and his royal friends, that still leaves 174 to be found... Even if you discount the supposed twelve vaults found by US operatives after World War II, it leaves one feeling extremely optimistic.

There are 7,107 islands in the Philippines. Depending on your point of view, this is either a bonus or a brick wall. So why not pick an island, hire a boat and go exploring – how hard can it be!

Just make sure you don't tell any corrupt politicians …

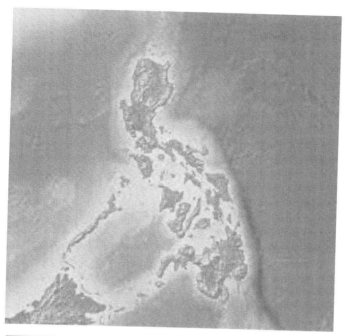

The beautiful Philippines are well worth a look anyway.

CHAPTER 7

The Kruger Millions

L et's go back to the year 1899 in South Africa. The Second Boer War, also known as the South African War, has begun in earnest. The conflict was fought between the British Empire and the 'Boers' – Afrikaans speaking South Africans descended from the Dutch East India Company's original settlers. Due to growing British presence and concerns over the future of their natural resources (gold and diamonds), the independent Boer Republics within South Africa, namely the Transvaal Republic and the Orange Free State, formed a militia and declared war on the British Empire on the 11th of October 1899.

The Transvaal (also known as the South African Republic), was led by President Paul Kruger, a religious and eccentric man said to be more suited to the 17th century, but a Boer through and through. Unfortunately for Kruger and the Boers, despite some surprising early success against one of the world's foremost military forces, the war was effectively over by 1900, as the Brits responded by dramatically increasing their troop numbers. Guerrilla tactics ensued until the official surrender in May of 1902, however President Kruger had left in exile in September of 1900.

Despite early successes, British resources proved too much for the Boer forces in the end.

Weeping as his train crossed the border into Mozambique, on his way to raise support for the Boer cause in Europe, Kruger had apparently concocted a plan to foil the British invaders; in economic terms at least. The Transvaal had become the richest nation in southern Africa after huge gold discoveries in 1886 – Kruger was not about to let the *Uitlanders* (foreigners – the Boer name for the British) get their hands on the republic's riches.

President Paul Kruger and a gold Kruger Ponde (Pound) from 1884.

Kruger had issued an order that should the British at any time threaten to reach the Transvaal capital of Pretoria, then the entire reserves of the national bank should be transported to the *veld* and hidden (the '*veld*' is the wide-open rural landscape typical to southern Africa).

On the 4ᵗʰ of June, 1900, under the cover of darkness, the Boer leaders made their escape from Pretoria by train, headed for the small Lowveld town of Machadodorp. From there they could continue to organise the resistance and escape via Mozambique if needed. Accompanying the ministers and soldiers, however, was another train, its compartments loaded with gold coins and bars – The Kruger Millions.

The following day the Brits under Lord Milner occupied Pretoria. The first order of business was to inspect the vaults of the national mint and bank – they were found empty. Reports collected by the British showed that between the 29ᵗʰ of May and the 4ᵗʰ of June in 1900, over $800,000 in

1-ounce gold 'Kruger Pounds' had been removed. Further investigation revealed the Transvaal government had been confiscating gold for months before the war began, as well as creating several thousand newly minted gold coins. A total of $2,000,000 in Kruger Pounds is said to be unaccounted for. Given an average annual inflation of 2.88% since 1900, the same amount would equal around **$80,000,000 US** in 2018.

The removal of the gold is corroborated by the Boer commander of Pretoria during the event, General J.C Smuts. Smuts states in his '*Memoirs of the Boer* War' that the Boer resistance held off the British just long enough to see the valuable cargo safely out of the city. This account is further backed up by Ernst Meyer, the Master of the South African Mint in 1900. Meanwhile, Kruger and other leading figures in the Boer War travelled by train through the town of Middelburg, onto Machadodorp and then Waterfal Boven towards Mozambique.

Map showing the various places through which President Kruger's train passed in 1900, carrying treasure, on its way to Lourenço Marques. It was into the country north of this line that some of the Republican treasure disappeared

The whereabouts of the gold train? Unknown. Kruger boarded a ship to France on the 19th of October, 1900 (apparently with as many gold coins as he could carry; think of politicians and their 'travel expenses'). The whereabouts of the train and its cargo, however, became subject to guesswork until a surprising turn of events a few years later.

On the 29th of September, 1905, a man named John Holtzhausen made a sworn declaration while in prison in the town of Kimberley, allegedly for stealing a horse and wagon. In an attempt no doubt to justify his crime, Holtzhausen claimed that during the war, he and two other men named Pretorius and Phillip Schwartz had received a direct order from the Kruger government. They were tasked with burying around $2 million worth of gold and diamonds, about 50 miles north of the Blyde River near Leydsdorp. Having completed the mission, Holtzhausen said that Pretorius had died in the war, and Schwartz had been hanged for murder. As luck would have it, Holtzhausen claimed he was on his way to retrieve the treasure when he was arrested. Hardly justification for stealing a horse and wagon, but worth a shot at freedom I guess. It's unknown what then happened to John Holtzhausen, like so many from past eras he simply disappeared from record.

Areas that keep appearing in research are usually around the province of Mpumalanga, in the north east of South Africa toward the border with Mozambique. Within Mpumalanga and also neighbouring Limpopo, places that have been mentioned include the rivers of Blyde and Elands, and the towns of Ermelo, Leydsdorp, Machadodorp, Waterval Onder (meaning 'over a waterfall') and Waterval Boven (meaning 'below a waterfall').

Picturesque Waterval Boven view from the train route, and below, an old section of the route probably used by the Boers towards their exile in Mozambique. Below right, an 1898 Kruger Ponde (Pound).

Found? Not Yet I Think...

Every few years someone else claims to have stumbled upon the Kruger Millions jackpot. In 2001 it was rumoured a family of Zulu labourers, whom had been living in the Ermelo region (eastern Mpumalanga) for over a hundred years, had at some point stumbled across 4,000 Kruger pounds, buried on a local farm. The family were said to have sold 400 of the coins over the past fifty years to supplement their income... Unlikely. If I find 4,000 gold coins, I'm not labouring another day in my life.

A headline as recently as 2016 documented a find in Emmarentia, a suburb of Johannesburg, the largest city in modern South Africa. Gerrie du Plooy was testing out a new kayak in Emmarentia Dam for his local canoe club when he capsized. In the process of going bottom-up, Gerrie saw something shiny on the dam floor. Thinking it was probably a watch, he dived down and made an awesome discovery – a heap of gold coins!

Unlike what many would have done, honest Gerrie immediately reported the find to the local council, who quickly organised a dive team to the site. The team apparently retrieved the 'small heap of gold coins', one of which was dated to 1892. It's unknown whether Gerrie's honesty was rewarded. This haul definitely does not match the description of the Kruger Millions. Rather it matches a small amount hidden by a local looking to safeguard his personal savings. Ergo – the Kruger Millions are still out there!

In the very least, the region in and around Mpumalanga is incredibly beautiful, home to some of South Africa's most picturesque tourist attractions. I plan to visit the waterfalls along the Blyde and Elands rivers and have a sniff around, you never never know if never never go to the Transvaal (with a spade).

CHAPTER 8

The Copper Scroll

One of the most important archaeological finds of the 20th century came between 1946-56 from the caves at Qumran, on the West Bank of the Jordan River and near the shores of the Dead Sea.

The discovery was initially made by Bedouin shepherds around 1946 when, after a goat had wondered into a cave, one of the Bedouin threw a stone into the cave to flush it out – then he heard the sound of something breaking. The shepherds found seven scrolls in ancient storage vases within the cave and, sensing the writings on the scrolls were of historical value, they tried to sell them off for a quick profit. Soon after, archaeologists got wind of the discovery and converged from across the globe. Over the next ten years, the area was scoured thoroughly, and a collection of no less than 981 different manuscripts were uncovered. These became renowned as the *Dead Sea Scrolls*.

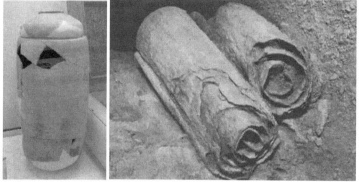

There are various theories as to how this library came to be scattered throughout caves in the area, and we do know a little about their intended purpose. For the most part, the scrolls contained Jewish religious texts and commentaries, were written at various times from the 8th century BCE onwards, used mostly Hebrew but also Aramaic and Greek, and were *mostly* written on parchment made from processed animal hide (vellum). I say *most*, because there is one scroll in particular that emerged made from copper – this is the scroll we are interested in.

The *Copper Scroll* was found on the 14th of March 1947, by archaeologists from the American Schools of Oriental Research (ASOR). The group were exploring the deepest parts of 'Cave 3' at Qumran and had already uncovered a trove of parchment and papyrus scrolls. There was one last scroll however, hidden at the back of the cave, and it soon became apparent that this discovery was unique. Immediately, the metallic substance distinguished it from all the other finds. This would prove also to be the characteristic that would hold the scroll's secret a while longer – the corroded metal could not be easily unrolled and the contents would remain hidden until a suitable method could be found to uncover her secrets.

In 1955, the decision was made to cut the Copper Scroll into 23 strips and then piece it back together. The excitement would have been through the roof as the experts laid out the pieces. The first thing they noticed was a language different from that of the other scrolls. It was definitely Hebrew but much closer to that of Mishnah (a major Jewish text, known as the 'oral Torah', written around 200 CE), rather than the more literal sounding Hebrew of the other scrolls. Ultimately, however, there was enough overlap with the orthography and palaeography of the existing scrolls to place the Copper Scroll at ca. 50-100 CE.

Working with the enthusiasm that comes from being at the edge of a great secret, the team transcribed the text and found yet another unique aspect. Unlike the majority of the Dead Sea Scrolls, the Copper Scroll was not a religious text, nor a commentary of ancient religious life - it appeared to be some kind of list or inventory.

A strip of the mysterious Copper Scroll, now housed at the Jordan Museum in Amman, Jordan.

What Type of Inventory?   The Gold and Silver Kind ...

In a stunning turn of events and contrary to all the other translations, the Copper Scroll turned out to be a *treasure map*. Sixty-four secret locations were detailed along with the amount in talents of gold and silver, gems and jars of coins that would be found there (a talent weighs around 33 kg). It has been estimated that there is a total of 4,600 talents of gold, silver and gemstones to be found – this amount could easily be worth in the **billions** of dollars today. One location alone is written to hold 900 talents of gold... that's a staggering **$1,247,400,000 US** at today's gold prices. *

So why haven't they been found?? Not to say there haven't been attempts to find the treasure, but there exist also a few additional reasons why she still lays hidden;

The clues are amazingly subtle. They appear to be simple directions, and therein lies the conundrum. It's as if you were to say, 'the gold is under my bed'. Only the author or someone who knows where your bed is could easily follow the directions. Having said this, there are numerous clues and place names within the scroll, as you'll see shortly.

Translation of the Copper Scroll is not as easy as the other religious related texts. There exists no precedent for the vocabulary used in the scroll, whereas there are religious texts existent or that can be referenced to similar works.

In terms of geopolitics, this lost treasure is perhaps the most flammable we are dealing with. I won't go into it too far here, but ever-present tensions in the middle-east, particularly over the land claims between Israel, Palestine and Jordan, would mean this particular area (Qumran), has been previously best left alone, especially in the case of a valuable archaeological find. That won't stop us from dreaming of treasure, or at least visiting the area also known for its hiking trails, Dead Sea floating, mudpacks and Masada sunrises (an incredible fortress built by Herod the Great atop a mountain).

Dead Sea sunrise view from Masada

An alternative definition of a 'talent' has also been translated from a scroll found in Cave 4 at Qumran. This puts the value of 1 talent at 6000 half-shekels, which are worth around $100 each today. This would still amount to $600,000 per talent.

Translations

Once the Copper Scroll was pieced back together, twelve columns of text were identified and have since been translated, albeit with the occasional nonsense due to a lack of transliteration, as you will see below (also note the presence of Greek characters written after certain passages – their meaning is thus far a mystery):

Column I

A Horebbah which is in the Vale of Achor under the stairs which go eastwards forty cubits; a box filled with silver weighing in all seventeen talents. KEN

In the tomb of ... the third: one hundred gold bars.

In the great cistern which is in the courtyard of the little colonnade, at its very bottom, closed with sediment towards the upper opening: nine hundred talents.

At the hill of Kohlit, containers, sandalwood and ephods (priestly garments). The total of the offering and of the treasure: seven talents and second tithe rendered unclean. At the exit of the canal on the northern side, six cubits towards the cavity of immersion. ΧΑΓ

In the hole of the waterproofed refuge, in going down towards the left, three cubits above the bottom; forty talents of silver.

Column II

In the cistern of the esplanade which is under the stairs: forty-two talents. HN

In the cave of the old Washer's House, on the third platform: sixty-five gold bars. OE

In the underground cavity which is in the courtyard of the House of Logs, where there is a cistern: vessels and silver, seventy talents.

In the cistern which is against the eastern gate, which is fifteen cubits away, there are vessels in it.

And in the canal which ends in it: ten talents.   ΔI

In the cistern which is under the wall on the eastern side, at the sharp edge of the rock: six silver bars; its entrance is under the large paving-stone.

In the pond which is east of Kohlit, at a northern angle, dig four cubits: twenty-two talents.

Column III

In the courtyard of ... in a southerly direction at nine cubits: silver and gold vessels of offering, bowls, cups, tubes, libation vessels. In all, six hundred and nine.

In the other, easterly direction dig sixteen cubits: forty talents of silver.   TP

In the underground cavity of the esplanade on its northern side: vessels of offering, garments. Its entrance is in the westerly direction.

In the tomb on the north-east of the esplanade three cubits under the trap: thirteen talents.

Column IV

In the great cistern which is in the ..., in the pillar on its northern side: fourteen talents.

In the canal which goes towards ... when you enter forty-one cubits: fifty-five talents of silver.

Between the two tamarisk trees in the Vale of Akhon, in their midst dig three cubits. There are two pots full of silver.

In the red underground cavity at the mouth of the 'Asiah: two hundred talents of silver.

In the eastern underground cavity to the north of the Kohlit: seventy talents of silver.

In the heap of stones of the valley of Sekhakha dig ... cubits: twelve talents of silver.

Column V

At the head of the water conduit ... at Sekhakha, on the northern side under the large ... dig three cubits: seven talents of silver.

In the split which is in Sekhakha in the east of the reservoir of Solomon; vessels of offering.

Quite close to them above the canal of Solomon sixty cubits towards the great stone dig three cubits: twenty-three talents of silver.

In the tomb which is in the wadi of Kippah going from Jericho to Sekhakha, at its entry from Jericho to Sekhakha, dig seven cubits: thirty-two talents.

Column VI

In the eastward looking cave of the Pillar with two entrances, dig at the northern entrance three cubits; there is a pitcher there, in it a book, under it twenty-two talents.

In the eastward looking cave of the base of the Stone dig nine cubits at the entrance: twenty-one talents.

In the Dwelling of the Queen on the western side dig twelve cubits: twenty-seven talents.

In the heaps of stones which is at the Ford of the High Priest dig nine cubits: twenty-two talents.

Column VII

In the water conduit of Q ... the greater northern reservoir, in the four directions measure out twenty-four cubits: four hundred talents.

In the nearby cave in the proximity of Bet ha-Qos dig six cubits: six silver bars.

At Doq under the eastern corner of the guard post dig seven cubits: twenty-two talents.

At the mouth of the water exit of Koziba dig three cubits towards the rock: sixty talents, two talents of gold.

Column VIII

In the water conduit on the road east of Bet Ahsor, which is east of Atizor, vessels of offering and books and a bar of silver.

In the outside valley ... at the stone dig seventeen cubits underneath: seventeen talents of gold and silver.

In the heap of stones at the mouth of the Pottery ravine dig three cubits: four talents.

In the westward looking stubble-field of ha-Sho, on the south side, at the underground chamber looking northwards dig twenty-four cubits: sixty-six talents.

In the irrigation of ha-Sho, at the stone sign in it, dig eleven cubits: seventy talents of silver.

Column IX

At the dovecot to the entrance of ha-Notef, measure out from its exit thirteen cubits, dig down under seven smooth stones: seven silver bars and four stater coins.

At 'Violet-Scarlet' over the eastward looking underground chamber dig eight cubits: twenty-three and a half talents of silver.

In the underground chambers of Horon, in the seaward looking underground chamber in the narrow part, dig sixteen cubits: twenty-two talents.

At Qob'ah a large amount of money and offerings.

At the 'sound of waters' close to the edge of the gutter on the east side of the exit dig seven cubits: nine talents.

In the underground cavity on the north side of the mouth of the gorge of Bet Tamar in the parched land of ... All that is in it is herem.

At the dovecot which is at Mesad, at the water conduit, southward at the second stair descending from the top: nine talents.

Column X

In the cistern next to the canals fed by the Great Wadi, at the bottom: twelve talents.

At the reservoir which is in Bet Kerem going to the left of ten notches: sixty-two talents of silver.

At the pond in the valley 'YK on its western side is a ma'ah coin coupled with two ma'ahs. This is the entrance: three hundred talents of gold and twenty pitched vessels.

Under the Hand of Absalom on the western side dig twelve notches: eighty talents.

At the pond of the privy of Siloa under the watering trough: seventeen talents.

At ... Jin the four angles: gold and vessels of offering.

Column XI

Next to them under the comer of the southern portico at the Tomb of Zadok under the pillar of the covered hall: vessels of offering of resin and offering of senna.

Next to them at the top of the westward looking rock towards the Garden of Zadok under the great closing stone which is at the conduit: devoted things.

In the tomb which is under the galleries: forty talents.

In the Tomb of the Sons of the Yerahite, in it: vessels of offering of cedar, offering of resin.

Next to them, at Bet Esh-Datain, in the reservoir where you enter the small pool: vessels of offering of aloes, and ...

Next to them, at the western entrance of the tomb is a channel over: nine hundred talents of silver and five talents of gold.

Column XII

Sixty talents at its entrance from the west under the black stone.

Near to them under the threshold of the sepulchral chamber: forty-two talents.

On Mount Gerizim under the stairs of the higher ground cavity: a box and its contents and sixty talents of silver.

In the great underground duct of the sepulchral chamber. The whole weighing seventy-one talents and twenty minas.

In the underground cavity which is in the smooth rock north of Kohlit, whose opening is towards the north with tombs at its mouth there is a copy of this writing and the measurements and details of each item.

A silver Jerusalem shekel from the time of the First Jewish - Roman War (AD 68).

Queen Sheba pays homage to King Solomon. Long before the Romans came onto the scene, Israel was rich and powerful, once ruled by the legendary King Solomon, said to be wealthy beyond imagination due to his famous mines.

Who Created the Copper Scroll and Buried Such Riches?

Here are a couple of my prime suspects:

The Sicarii of the famed last stand at Masada. At the end of the First Jewish – Roman War (66 – 73 CE), a group of 967 Sicarii, a diehard faction of the Jewish Zealots, took refuge atop the fortress of Masada, over-looking the western shores of the Dead Sea. The Sicarii had previously crushed the 700 strong Roman garrison that had taken residence in former King Herod's palace fortress at Masada, and now reserved the seemingly impregnable mountain top for their final action. Having been surrounded for six months by the Roman legions of Lucius Flavius Silva, the Sicarii had watched as the Romans used Jewish slave labour to build an enor-mous rampart capable of reaching the cliff top walls of the previously insurmountable fortress. Rather than await the Romans and face certain death or worse (slavery), the Sicarii are reported by historian Flavius Jo-sephus to have committed a mass suicide, burning half of their food sup-plies before the act (to prove they could have survived longer and faced the Roman attack, but had the courage to leave the world on their terms – only two women and five children are said to have survived). Due to their freedom or death attitude, the Sicarii were not the most popular of the Jewish sects, often attacking less 'enthusiastic' countrymen who did not agree with their point of view (700 Jewish villagers slain at nearby Ein Gedi were proof of their extremism). All the same, they are a good fit to have authored the copper scrolls, they fit the supposed date of manufac-ture (50 – 100 CE), they were definitely active in the region, and would certainly not have let such treasures easily fall into the hands of their Ro-man foes (there were multiple occasions when the Roman governors had plundered the treasury of the Jewish temple to punish minor Jewish upris-ings, actions that ironically would later contribute to larger revolts).

Simon bar Kokhba, the Judaean leader of The Third Jewish – Roman War (c. 132 – 135 CE), also known as the Bar Kokhba Revolt. The revolt yielded early victories for the Jews and lead to a three-year reign for Bar Kokhba, before the Romans severely defeated the Judeans under Emperor Hadrian. Along with heavy Roman military losses, the war reportedly left more than 580,000 Jews dead, as well as the destruction of fifty fortified towns and 985 villages. In an effort to erase Israel and Judaea from history, Hadrian renamed the region Syria Palestina and banned Jews from Jerusalem.

In 1953 at Nahal Hever in the Judaean Desert, about forty kilometres south of Qumran and ten kilometres north of Masada, Bedouin tribesman found what became known as the Cave of Letters. Usually not associated with the Dead Sea Scroll finds, the discovery included several letters of correspondence and instructions from Bar Kokhbah to his generals. The time line is a good enough match, Simon bar Kokhba would have had the available resources, and the geography is also solid.

Where Do We Start Our Search?

As you can judge by the translations above, the Copper Scroll was designed to be read (and understood) by someone with intimate knowledge of the locations described. Sure, there appear to be locations, but there are no coordinates or *definite* points of reference, only the familiar descriptions of local areas as they were perhaps named two thousand years ago, be they within a city, town or village. Unless one can find the final location mentioned in Column XII, which apparently deciphers the scroll, the process of elimination must begin. There are many ancient dwellings in the area, from continually inhabited cities such as Jerusalem and Jericho, to smaller abandoned ancient sites.

You must research the cryptic messages within the scroll. There are place names galore that may today go by a different or varied name (for example, from Column XI, *'Bet Esh-Datain'* as a location is a good likeness to *'Bethesda' – Check out the Pools of Bethesda in Jerusalem and you'll see more than just a name connection).*

There are alternative translations available that appear to solve much of the scroll, such as the one by Hack and Carey, but it's up to you how to approach this mystery; perhaps with a little research and a fresh set of eyes you will decipher the secrets of the Copper Scroll on your own.

As a starting point and in addition to the magnificent Jerusalem (not only are there possible connections within the Copper Scroll to the ancient city, but it is quite simply an awe-inspiring location), below are five ancient settlements you may want to consider.

Jerusalem - The Holiest of Cities. Surrounded by ancient walls, centred by the Temple Mount (Dome of the Rock in Islam) and pivotal to the three great monotheistic faiths, the ancient citadel is rich in history and secrets.

Khirbet Midras

Used during the Bar Kokhbah revolt, the Khirbet Midras location contains a system of tunnels and caves, a columbarium (a storage place for funerary urns), a burial pyramid and later a Byzantine church. The complex is located within the Adullum Grove Nature Reserve in central Israel, the nearest city being Beit Shemesh.

Betar

The name 'Betar' means 'fortress', and in this case was the last Jewish fort held during Simon Bar Kokhbar's revolt against the Romans (135 CE). Located in the present-day West Bank area south-west of Jerusalem, the decimation of Betar by Hadrian's army was said to be of biblical proportions. After a three-and-a-half-year siege, the Jewish population of Betar met a sad end at the hands of the relentless Romans - but maybe they managed to hide their wealth well enough so the invaders wouldn't get their hands on it.

Masada

As mentioned above, the clifftop fortress built by King Herod the Great, and later occupied by the Sicarii prior to their defiant exit in 73 CE. The magnificent Masada is perched 400 metres above the Dead Sea, making for the most imperious sunrises in Israel. She measures 550 x 270 metres, and is home to a palace, barracks, armoury, bathhouses, store rooms, a synagogue, a Byzantine church and enormous cisterns that were ingeniously dug from the mountain to hold rainwater. There is easily enough infrastructure to satisfy the descriptions given in the Copper Scroll, including the numerous references to 'cisterns', 'gates' and 'pools'.

Masada - Herod's spectacular palace / fortress overlooking the Dead Sea.

Qumran

Dated to around 100 BCE, the ancient settlement of Qumran is of interest for an obvious reason - it is the closest known settlement to the Qumran Caves; home of the Dead Sea and Copper Scrolls. Qumran has been known to archaeologists since 1851, but excavations only began in earnest in 1949 after a connection was drawn to the nearby caves of the Dead Sea Scrolls.

The settlement contained numerous cisterns, Jewish ritual baths, a cemetery (in which over 1000 bodies were buried) and other infrastructure which has led to varied speculation. Theories include Qumran as a fort, a religious commune (of the Essenes sect – a perennial favourite as authors of the Dead Sea Scrolls), a wealthy family's retreat and even a production centre of ceramics. It is quite possible Qumran was a combination of all of the above but appears to have been destroyed by the Romans around the same time that they decimated Masada (68 – 73 CE).

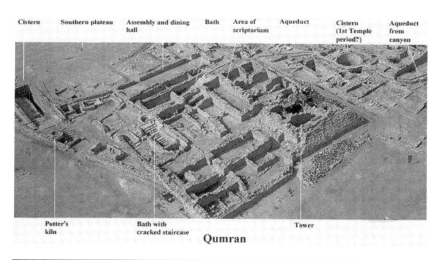

Qumran

Ein Gedi

The famous oasis is these days found in a designated nature reserve, close to Masada, Qumran and the Dead Sea. Given its importance as a water source, it's no surprise Ein Gedi has been inhabited since Neolithic times, and is referenced by Josephus Flavius as being a village sacked by the Sicarii from Masada, during which the 700 hundred inhabitants were massacred. As recently as 1999, Ein Gedi was excavated by archaeologists and became known as the 'Essenes' site, a good connection with the alleged authors of the Dead Sea Scrolls.

A synagogue mosaic has survived from Ein Gedi's past, upon which an inscription is written in Juedo-Aramaic. The inscription warns the local inhabitants against *'revealing the town's secret'* – Could it be a reference to treasure locations recorded in the Copper Scroll?

The heavenly Oasis at Ein Gedi.

Head to the Holy Land

What are you waiting for? Decipher the Copper Scroll – it is full of clues that can and have been interpreted a thousand ways, now it's your turn. When you're done in the library, book a flight and head off to the Holy Land on a quest to uncover ancient riches, but remember, *it belongs in a museum!*

CHAPTER 9

The Golden Owl

Falling into the same genre as the *Fenn Treasure*, the *Golden Owl is real*, and it is a small fortune within your reach. Buried in a secret location somewhere in France, the treasure has been lying in wait for over twenty-five years, seekers as yet unable to successfully decipher the cryptic clues left by her creator.

The treasure was the brainchild of Max Valentin (real name Regis Hauser). For decades Valentin had toyed with the idea of hiding a treasure, then providing a riddle or cipher that, once cracked, would lead the worthy hunter to their prize. So it was, in partnership with designer and artist Michael Becker, that Valentin created eleven cryptic clues that would lead to a buried bronze owl, which in turn could be redeemed for an owl made of pure gold and silver with a head covered in diamonds.

At 3.30 am on the 24th of April in 1993, Valentin buried the bronze owl at an undisclosed location, somewhere in France at a depth of two metres. A month later he and Becker published *Sur la Trace de la Chouette D'or (On the Trail of the Golden Owl)*, containing an illustrated double page spread for each of the eleven clues – the hunt for the Golden Owl had officially begun.

She's buried somewhere in there...

Value?

The Owl is currently vaulted with a bailiff named Master Llouquet in Paris. She is 25 cm in height, 50 cm wide and weighs 15 kg. She was valued at $1,000,000 Francs in 1994, equal to €250,000 Euros today, with an additional appraisal by a Swiss collector suggesting three times this amount – is this incentive enough for you to invest in a spade?

The Creators

Max Valentin (Regis Hauser) and Michael Becker are the men behind the creation of the Golden Owl hunt. An idea in the works since the 1970s, it apparently took Valentin around 500 hours to create the aforementioned eleven riddles, and then publish *Sur la Trace de la Chouette D'or* with his business partner, who in the meantime had created the precious statuette. Valentin estimated that it would take treasure hunters around four to six months to solve the riddles and find the Golden Owl. Much to his surprise, years passed and the puzzle remained a puzzle. By the time he met his end in a car crash in 2009, no one had yet solved the Golden Owl mystery – this is despite Valentin creating a further twenty treasure hunts in the meantime, all of which had been completed by the time he passed away. The Golden Owl remained the only quest yet to be completed, a haunting legacy to its mastermind.

It has been reported that in 2011, Michael Becker attempted to claim sole ownership of the Golden Owl, in order to sell her and recoup financial losses accumulating from the expenses of the quest (fair enough). However, two judicial decisions have apparently stopped this from taking place – the hunt is still on.

A Golden Owl (not ours); unfortunately, the creators have copyrighted images of the original, but you can easily find them online.

The Riddle

The entire riddle for this quest is contained within the published twenty-two-page book, *Sur la Trace de la Chouette D'or*. The book consists of eleven double-page spreads, each containing a title, a riddle and an illustration. Furthermore, each pair of pages is marked with a number apparently associated with the wavelength of its colours (representing the colour of visible light ranging from 700 nm at the red end to 400 nm at the violet end), along with the image of an owl. One look at the content of the riddles and you may understand why the Owl remains under earth still – at first glance she appears a mighty daunting task. However, after several hours reading the cryptic lines, cross referencing maps, theories and existing hypotheses, you *will* form the premise for your own search. Unfortunately, I can only share the book's words here (not the imagery), but a simple web search will give you a chance to study the publication, complete with illustrations.

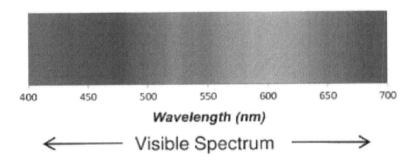

Without further ado, the riddles of the Golden Owl:

Page Number & Wavelength	Title and Riddle
1 - 500	**UT QUEANT LAXIS** At 2424-42-424-44-224-24-42-24, take the orthogonal. To find the spiral with four centres, 560.606 measures, it's far. But by the Mega, it's a million times less.
2 - 530	**OPENING** My first, first half of the half of the first age, Precedes my Second and Third, seeking their way. My Fourth is inspired, my Fifth is in rage, But, without protest, follows my Fourth and the roman alpha. My Sixth is hidden at the limits of ETERNITY. My Seventh, standing, spits his venom. To find my all, just to be wise,

	Because the Truth, in truth, will not be a Devin's affair.
3 - 780	**FIRST STEP...** Wherever you want, By the ross and the coachman. But where you have to, By the compass and the foot.
4 - 600	**WHEN AL-MAR ALLIES TO PRAENESTE FIBULA, DARKNESS SHINE** BDI,J. DF,F. CFD. BJ. HJ. EA,B. BC. E. DC,B. CDI,B. BAB,H. BE. CD. FB. BCG,J. BIG,D. BE. BG. BJD,B. DB. BGH,C. BC. E.
5 - B	**THERE IS NO WORSE BLIND PEOPLE THAN THE ONE THAT DOES NOT WANT TO SEE** 1 = 530 3 = 470 5 = 600 7 = 420 9 = 650

6 - 420	**FROM THE SKY COMES THE LIGHT** 365-HI-10752 I-10752 WHERE 365-HE EAGLE 90677-RI-60140-365-ED 365-HE 687-ARK OF HI-10752 CLAW-10752 I-60140 365-HE 10752-ABLE, O-60140-E H-30667-60140-DRED DAY-10752 BEFORE BREAKI-60140-G HI-10752 BEAK A-60140-D LOO-10752-I-60140-G HI-10752 FEA-365-HER-10752 Then lend a bow to Apollo: from this point, he will count 1969,697 measures towards the zenith. In a fraction of a 46,241,860th of a sidereal day, his line will fall. Hasten to find the arrow.
7 - 520	**EARTH OPENS** Between them, there would be only two intervals if they were aligned. But this would be a too easy game! Now that you have undone all the

	yarns,
	    Doubt is the last torment that will be inflicted to you.
	    Because it is the rule of this cruel game:
	    Alone, you have to find where to land your shovel.
	    Show your respect for Mother Nature,
	    And before getting away, close its injury.

8 - 650	**WHEN ALL IS REVEALED**
	    Back to the Ponant, seeks the Sentinels.
	    At 8000 measures from there, they are waiting for you.
	    Find them, you need to review them.

9 - 470	**IT'S THE RIGHT WAY IF THE ARROW TARGETS THE HEART**
	    My First multiplies by gaiety.
	    My Second offers you space,
	    My Third air, and my Fourth water.
	    When he's lying, my Fifth snores.
	    My Sixth is worth one hundred, and my Seventh is just one node.
	    My Eighth tastes like laurel,

While my Ninth, with astonishment, stays behind.

My Tenth is always naked when there's a link.

My Eleventh, finally, is the unknown.

Found my all, and through the opening, you will see the light.

10 - 560

AD AUGUSTA PER ANGUSTA

When at Carusburc, you will have Albion in the back,

Seek the opening that reveals the Heavenly Light.

Don't linger, don't ask for your rest,

But prepare yourself to walk on water.

Twice, Neptune will help you

And carry you away from the icy north.

Pursue your road and do not interrupt your journey

Before seeing, through the Opening, the becalmed Nave.

Without deviating an inch, draw a line,

And you will not regret what you did.

11 - 580	**THE GOOD WAY, IT IS THE WAY OF THE OPPOSITE WAY, AND VICE VERSA** 19.9.13.12.15.19.18.21.15.9.19 will be worth 1 12.15.19.18.21.15.9.19.18.9.13.8.15.4 will be worth 2 9.13.16.16.9.13.9.5.18 will be worth 3 25.1.12.14.18.9.13.16.9.13 will be worth 4 8.15.4.1.12.9.19.18.15.1.6 will be worth 5 18.9.13.13.5.18.18.1.12.18.9.13.12.15.19 will be worth 6 20.18.21.15.15.4.9.18.9.13.8 will be worth 7 9.13.18.9.15.19.19.9 will be worth 8 15.4.1.12.14.18.1.12.10 will be worth 9 19.18.9.13.12.15.19.14.1.12 will be worth 0

Extra Clues from Max Valentin

Perhaps frustrated with the time being taken to solve his masterpiece, and after hosting a web server for eight years that he claims answered over 100,000 queries, Max Valentin dropped a few hints to aid hunters in their Golden Owl quest:

- *The Owl is buried at least 62 miles inland, and only Valentin knows the spot (knew the spot).*

- *The Owl is not on an island (effectively ruling out Mont Saint-Michel and Notre Dame de Paris; popular theories before they were dispelled by Valentin).*

- *Not on private property – be it open to the public or not.*

- *Not buried in Paris, Versailles or the 'Dark Forest' (possibly the legend-filled Paimpont Forest in Brittany).*

To reach the final 'zone', the hunter must use a map of some sort, then utilise a more precise map of that zone to pinpoint the Owl's burial place.

There is a 'mega-trick' in existence that provides the key to sequencing the eleven riddles that lead to the final zone.

Upon reaching the final zone, the hunter will need to discover and solve a final riddle, one that can be solved using the contents of the previous twelve riddles and will ultimately lead to the prize.

In 1995, Valentin hypothesised that hunters had collectively solved around ninety-five percent of the riddles, but that a lack of collaboration was keeping them from the final hurdle. Also, in the same year, Valentin checked on the Owl and ensured it was still buried, noting that disturbed earth 120 metres from the location could have been by hunters ever so close…

In 1996, Valentin stated that the 'remainders' are the key to finding the Owl, and that they can be found in the ten riddles that are marked by a wavelength number.

She is buried at a depth of two metres and covered with stones and earth (putting her out of range of most recreational metal detectors).

Popular Theories

A popular location doing the rounds is the commune of Dabo, situated in the Moselle region of north-east France. Due to connections within the riddle to the '500 spiral found on the precise map' and the 'height of the Apollo arrow', many have been to the region with hope in their hearts. Also, Dabo was identified around the same time as Notre Dame de Paris and Mont-Saint Michel, and while the latter two were summarily dismissed by Valentin, he gave no indication of Dabo's exclusion.

Theories abound regarding Becker's detailed illustrations in Sur la Trace de la Chouette D'or. Numerous hidden objects and figures have been extracted, including hands, eyes, gods, tools and even submarines. It's all very open to interpretation, for a picture may tell a thousand words, but are they merely decoration?

A self-described 'new-comer' to treasure hunting boldly announced in 2015 that he had solved all the riddles, right down to the final zone location of the Owl (and in doing so openly mocking those who had come before him). The ingenious solution (self-proclaimed) involved organizing the eleven riddles by the order of the wavelengths of light featured on each page:

B, 420, 470, 500, 520, 530, 560, 580, 600, 650, 780.

Mr. Genius then 'reads' them and discovers the zone. According to this gentleman, the riddle employs the concepts of darkness and light, and that there are five parts as follows:

"Original Order", "B Order", "Light Order", "Super Solution Part I (the final zone)", and "Super Solution Part II (dig here for the Owl).

An interesting interpretation, however as of 2018, the Owl remains at rest.

French Treasure, Cheese and Wine ... Wine Not?

For the original disciples of this adventure, twenty-five years is a long time to have pondered the cache of the Golden Owl. I look forward to having my own stab in the dark, saving up for a week in France and joining the chase. In doing so leave no doubt I will be tasting some of that famous French wine and cheese, all the while taking in the beautiful country side as I too ponder a spot to dig two metres down (hopefully without striking electrical cables). If I happen to find an owl that I can swap in Paris for a quarter of a million euros? Well... that would be very nice.

CHAPTER 10

Trabuco's Gold

I'm sure we've all fantasised about a get rich quick scheme at some point in our lives, but one group of Mexican millionaires fixed to make this dream a reality, and they created a treasure horde of gold for us in the process. This is their story.

On the fifth of April, 1933, in the wake of the Great Depression, the United States government decided drastic measures needed to be taken to save their economy. President Roosevelt issued an executive order concerning the US Gold Standard (the monetary system in which the value of the currency is directly linked to the price of gold) - it would become illegal for US citizens to horde or own gold, and only refineries and miners would be able to sell to the federal mints. This order was in advance of the proposed Gold Act which would enable the government to control the supply and value of gold, including setting a higher price on the commodity to improve the US economy.

However, the law still had to pass through the formalities of government, and in the meantime a few savvy Mexican investors caught wind of the proposal, deciding that they could profit from the changes. On the 15th of April 1933, a meeting took place in Cuenavaca, a little town cradled in the mountains south of Mexico City.

The Plan

To set the scene, picture a group of wealthy Mexican businessmen holding a clandestine summit in the mountains. In attendance were Leon Trabuco - a miner and rancher from the Chihuahua district (a man with tonnes of gold already stored), Carlos Sepulvada – a rancher from Coahuila district, Ricardo Artega – a rancher from Torreon, Rafael Borega – an international banker and finance expert on Europe and North America, and finally an academic known only as Professor Morado from the economic department of the University of Mexico.

Backed by the Professor, the meeting began with Borega presenting evidence that the US would likely set a gold standard at least $10 above the existing price of $20.67 per ounce. The plan was simple, buy up gold in Mexico (much of which could be obtained for an even lower price from unregulated miners and suppliers), smuggle it across the border, wait for the US government to set a higher price, sell the gold to make a thirty percent profit and Roberto's your Uncle. It was definitely still a gamble, but the group were convinced they could move the gold easily, and the windfall would be a golden opportunity too good to pass up.

The inevitable question arose before the meeting concluded; 'What if we can't sell the gold?' This was not to be an issue; the group would find a buyer somewhere within the capitalist United States. They had done it before and they'd do it again.

Leon Trabuco would be putting up the lion's share of gold and would also be in charge of transport to and storage within the US, hence the group became known as the 'Trabuco Group'.

The Buy Up

With the decision made, the group needed to get its hands on as much gold as they could before the price went up. Trabuco put in eight tonnes he had stored already, Artega added four tonnes, and then Sepulvada provided the investment for Borega to buy up five more tonnes through mainly unregulated suppliers, thereby obtaining bargain prices and avoiding the federal paper trail. By the end of 1933, the Trabuco Group had amassed seventeen tonnes of stamped 99% gold and made haste to move it across the border before the gold price rose.

The Smuggle

In August of 1933, having obtained deer hunting permits and under the premise of visiting family in the States, Trabuco and two trusted employees drove a Dodge truck across the border at Nogales. Driving through Arizona to the New Mexico Four Corners area, the trio had no problem registering their rifles and obtaining visitor visas.

Trabuco scouted the land for a suitable place to land a small plane. Somewhere north-west of Shiprock, he found a good spot on a mesa top, with a 360-degree view and steep cliffs on three sides, and then marked out a strip to ensure a safe landing. Trabuco then learned from locals at the nearby town of Farmington, that there were crop dusting crews that would come to the area during the summer months from Salt Lake City for work. Making contact with a crew, Trabuco obtained the details of their best flyer, a man named Bill Elliot (also known as Red Moiser by some sources). Elliot owned a Stearman plane with modifications in order to carry heavier loads and large fuel tanks for longer journeys. The pilot was convinced to fly out for a meeting near Kirkland, New Mexico.

Stearman crop dusting planes, also known to be full of gold ingots.

Shiprock, San Juan County, New Mexico (read on, but I bet this is the 'landmark' later mentioned by Trabuco).

Trabuco and Elliot made a deal. Elliot, whose work in the fields had ended for the season, was to be supplied fuel, provisions and $2500 per flight from Chihuahua to the secret landing site. A bonus of five percent of the profits from the future gold sales was added to encourage discretion.

The pilot from Utah and the businessman from Mexico then flew Elliot's Stearman south to meet the other partners and to authorise future pickups. They then returned to New Mexico with their first load of just under one tonne of gold. They were met by Trabuco's trusted employees who had set up a camp in the isolated region and were conducting patrols on horseback to ensure secrecy was maintained. The men had set up landing site towers with rocks from old Indian hogans nearby (traditional Navajo houses). One of these hogans had a sunken ground floor which the transported gold was temporarily placed into, then covered with a tarp and sand.

Between August and November 1933, Elliot set to work secretly flying seventeen tonnes of gold into the US. With each five tonnes that would accumulate (every third flight), Trabuco would return and load one tonne each time into a pick-up truck, then set off in an easterly direction from the Indian hogan site. Witnesses say Trabuco would take about one hour to complete the round-trip to the hiding place. Elliot completed ten flights to New Mexico and the whole seventeen tonnes of gold had been safely smuggled into the US. It was said that Trabuco greatly enjoyed this secret venture and its clandestine nature.

The Price Prophecy Comes True – This Might Just Work

On the 17th of January 1934, the US Gold Act was approved. Forthwith, all banks, refineries and brokers were ordered to turn in their gold to federal mints, in exchange for US Dollars at the new price of $35 per ounce. At the same time, it was ordered that private citizens who retained gold would be subject to illegal storage law violations. The Trabuco Group was over the moon, it was as Professor Morada had predicted; only it would not be easy to sell, as the only legal buyers were now the federal mints... The group convened and heard the Professor's advice (he was convinced the price would rise higher still), then the four financial members of the group voted on whether to sell or hold their gold. Borega and Sepulvada voted to sell at least enough to recoup their investments, while Trabuco was given power over Artega's vote, and upon deciding not to sell thus produced a stalemate. In order to avoid a split in the group, Trabuco reluctantly agreed to travel to the US and explore options to sell.

Sell! Sell! Sell! ... But How?

Trabuco soon learned in Denver that no private broker would buy their gold – the government had been true to their policy (for a change). He presented a plan to the group back in Mexico - they would file a mining claim and falsify records so that they could then sell to the federal mints; the sale would be conducted by a trusted Latino / US citizen they would recruit and reward for his loyalty (effectively adding yet another partner). This method would take time, but if they tried to sell the whole stash at once it would appear on the tax man's radar and draw unwanted attention, requiring a deeper and deeper pit of lies. It would be a slow liquidation, but their options now appeared limited.

US President Franklin D Roosevelt signing something in 1933 (may or may not have been the Gold Act, which would come to be a major 'pain in the Trabuco' due to one important and unforeseen condition that prevented an easy sale).

One by One They Fall

It was by now 1939, and plans were made to offload the gold through a US citizen. Borega disagreed, claiming he could move the gold to Germany if Trabuco could get it back to Mexico.

Rafael Borega, the international investment banker who had called the first group meeting in Cuenavaca, then died of heart failure in his office in July of that year.

Trabuco approached the German embassy in Mexico but was suspected of being a spy for the US, and was politely asked to leave. Given the events that proceeded 1939 in Germany it was probably for the best that the gold wasn't moved there.

Carlos Sepulvada, the rancher from Coahuila responsible for procuring five tonnes of the gold, died in a drunk driving accident outside Monterey, Mexico in 1940.

Trabuco turned to Bill Elliot, the pilot who was patiently waiting for his share of the profit. Elliot seemed like a good candidate to sell the gold; he was a US citizen and he was already in on the deal. However, feeling the patriotic call, Elliot enlisted as a fighter pilot in World War II; he was shot down and killed over Germany in 1944.

There is no further mention of Ricardo Artega, whether he became a silent partner or passed away is unclear. In any case he trusted Trabuco, as evidenced by giving him his vote in previous meetings. All further investigations reference only Leon Trabuco, seemingly the sole guardian of seventeen tonnes of Mexican gold buried somewhere on United States soil.

Desperation Leads to an Investigation

Sensing the need to walk away from what was becoming a disastrous business venture (and having kindly reimbursed Carlos Sepulvada's relatives for his losses), Trabuco tried again and again to sell the gold to private buyers in the US. Unfortunately, no one would budge and the US Treasury Department was informed; an investigation began and I'm sure Leon was wishing he'd kept his gold at home.

In 1946, accused of violating the Gold Act and US smuggling laws, Trabuco was offered the chance to prove ownership of the gold in the US Federal Court, but first he would need to come forward, answer the charges and reveal the hiding place of the seventeen tonnes. Sensing a trap, Trabuco declined the invitation and decided not to chance a return to the United States any time soon. The case stalled and was handed to the Federal Grand Jury in 1952.

Seemingly looking to avoid trouble and enjoy his retirement, Trabuco sold up his ranches and his mines in Mexico, opting for a Mediterranean diet in Spain instead. Maintaining contact with his attorneys in Los Angeles, Trabuco made sporadic inquiries on the progress of the case against him (and whether or not it had expired). The last known inquiry was in 1974; Leon Trabuco would have been eighty-six years old. The outcome of the case has never been made public, as far as we know the leader of the Trabuco Group died in comfort in Spain, though no doubt with a pinch of regret that he was never able to regain his golden fortune from the sands of New Mexico.

An Obsession Fostered

Although nothing more is recorded in history of Leon Trabuco, and the only clue allegedly uttered by the man was *'The gold is only a few miles from a major New Mexico landmark'*, many have tried to pick up the trail and unearth his hidden bounty. The foremost of these seekers was a man named Ed Foster. A Farmington local, Foster spent over thirty-five years of his life searching for the gold. He knows the area and he knows the locals – some who remember as far back as the 1930s.

Foster interviewed a local Ute Indian woman who recalls not only the plane from when she was a child (it would have been an odd occurrence on the reservation), but also the Mexican men living on the land under Trabuco's instructions (an even stranger occurrence for the locals).

Having searched the land for so many years, Foster believes he has not only located the mesa that was used as a landing strip, known on maps as 'Conger Mesa', but also a Mexican style house about twenty miles to the west of the mesa. This house is distinctly foreign and definitely out of place on an Indian reservation.

On a rocky outcrop in the area, Foster claims to have found an engraving that reads:

'1933 - 16 ton'.

He nicknamed this spot 'Shrine Rock', and believes the treasure lies somewhere within the triangle that connects the engraving, Conger Mesa and the Mexican style house.

Ed Foster's last words on the location of the gold?

'I have looked with my eyes and metal detectors for many years. And now they have technology, and that's why I think it's going to be found, with technology. It's not gonna be found with dumb luck, because I've spent all of that.'

Silver Lining

I would hope that Ed Foster's metal detector was faulty, and maybe he has given us a head start to find the gold. It would be worth a trip to see the spectacular scenery I've so far only seen in films of the Wild West. There is however, a silver lining, an additional incentive besides the view, and it comes to us from a most surprising source – the Jesuit Order priests no less.

That's right, when Spain was still running its colonies in the New World, including the areas in and around what is now New Mexico, many mines were worked under the direction of the Jesuit Order. However, their expulsion in 1767 caused the sudden closure of the mines, the locations of which were hidden, in the hope Spain would reclaim control of their empire. As we know, this never happened, and the rich silver mines are also out there, waiting to be stumbled upon, perhaps while you are in the midst of hunting down Trabuco's Gold. Saddle-up and Buena Suerte!

Printed in Great Britain
by Amazon

66345056R00084